LOOKING FORWA
BEING ATTACKED

Return to Marjie Alger

1438 El Monte Dr

Thousand Oaks 91362

805-495-6380 V/TT

LOOKING FORWARD TO BEING ATTACKED

Self-Protection for Every Woman

By
LIEUTENANT JIM BULLARD
Memphis Police Department

Edited by
CRAIG COWLES

Photographs by
NOEL BARROW

M. EVANS AND COMPANY, INC.   New York

Library of Congress Cataloging-in-Publication Data

Bullard, Jim.
  Looking forward to being attacked.

  1. Self-defense for women. I. Cowles, Craig.
II. Title.
GV1111.5.B84   1987   613.6′6′024042   87–8945

ISBN 0–87131–500–9

M. Evans and Company, Inc.
216 East 49 Street
New York, New York 10017

Design by Lauren Dong

Manufactured in the United States of America

9 8 7 6 5 4 3 2 1

Table of Contents

PREFACE

In 1969, the chief of the Memphis Police Department directed me to develop a thirty-minute public demonstration that would teach women self-defense techniques which they could use to ward off attackers.

In those demonstrations, which were indeed good public relations for our police department, I concentrated on displaying one of the first martial art self-defense principles. Anyone can escape an attacker's grip simply by applying pressure against its weakest point.

After several presentations in which I led question and answer sessions, it became evident that the average woman would not benefit from a more extensive self-defense program unless she experienced an accompanying attitude change toward her attacker. It appeared that every woman I met was prone to imagine the typical attacker as being some master criminal with superior physical strength and intellectual powers. Of course, this is totally untrue.

It was at one of these early demonstrations that a young woman asked to speak to me privately. As she related an attack which had happened to her a few years earlier, she began to shake visibly and tears crested in her eyes. Her story, as told in Chapter One, proved to me that she personified the typical victim in this country and I knew that I could give her private self-defense lessons for fifteen years yet she would still be the victim of any attack. She was preconditioned to be the victim.

From that point, the demonstration took on a new meaning for me. It was no longer primarily a public relations gimmick. My message became as pertinent to men as to women and that message is the key point in this book as well as the key point to survival in this country. Each of us must change our attitude toward being attacked. Since we have not been successful in hiding from aggression, we must meet it head on and without fear.

Look forward to being attacked, not with fear, but with a properly controlled, well-channeled response of outrage and anger.

CHAPTER ONE

You'll Never Enjoy Being Attacked If You Don't Change Your Attitude!

The delightful subject of this book is your being attacked: attacked on the street, in a parking lot, in an elevator, in your car, in your bedroom, in the library's social science section, in your dentist's office. Wherever you are in today's social climate, you are subject to attack—which is terrific, because when you are finished with this book, you are going to be looking forward to being attacked!

You will have so many wonderful surprises in store for your attacker that the pleasure will be all yours the next time you are attacked. However, I am talking about your being attacked by a stranger, not a husband or boyfriend. I'm sorry to inform you that it is a lot easier to defend yourself from a stranger than from a husband or boyfriend. These movements will work against loved ones, but seem more easily applied against strangers. The simple reason for this is that while your husband, boyfriend, uncles and even neighbors may know your defenses, strangers do not. So most importantly, do not tell your attacker what you are going to do. The element of surprise is the most important part of your defense. Let everything you do to your attacker be a surprise to him. You'll love it!

Now, you are not going to enjoy being attacked unless you have the right attitude. More than anything else, your attitude will determine whether or not you are the victim of the attack to which you are subjected. There is very little that you can do about being the subject of an attack, but there is a big difference between being the subject of an attack and being the victim of that attack. The attitude you must adopt is that you will not let anyone spoil even three minutes of your day. This attitude is an important element in your defense. All the self-defense techniques in this book will not be of much benefit if you "short-circuit down the middle of your very being." Take offense every time offended—react in anger, not in fear. Channel anger in a positive direction and it will work for your self-defense. Fear is crippling but anger will give you strength of courage to do what you have to do. Let me illustrate this important point by relating an incident recently reported to the police.

The police report stated the attack took place on a busy downtown street around 1:00 P.M. There was motor traffic as well as pedestrian traffic present. The victim had been bruised by the strength of the attacker's grip on her arm just above her elbow. The victim had lost ten dollars from her purse. Her injury was slight and the financial loss insignificant, but she is the classic victim.

The woman told police that as she was returning to work from having eaten lunch, she suddenly suspected she was being followed. The farther she walked, the more intense the suspicion became. She never could force herself to turn around to see if she truly was being followed. She reported that when she stopped for the traffic signal, the attacker walked up beside her and grabbed her arm. He got her attention immediately! As soon as he seized her, the skin surfacing her elbow broke. During the next three weeks, a bruise radiated from her armpit to her wrist.

He pushed her out of the line of walking traffic, then held her in place while he calmly opened her purse with his free hand. After rummaging through the purse until he found her billfold, he took the billfold, put it in his pocket, looked her straight in the eyes, and thanked her with an obscenity. He pushed her aside then calmly turned and walked away, leaving her standing on the corner with her mouth and purse hanging open. There she stood until a passer-by noticed her unusual state and asked if anything was wrong. She said that she heard him but couldn't even answer. He saw her struggling within herself so he took it upon himself to touch her on the arm and ask again if he could help her. Well, his gentle touch and tone set off the fireworks. She screamed and raised such a hysterical fuss that she attracted a crowd which almost attacked the fellow who had come to her aid, thinking him to be the attacker.

The woman described her attacker as being a large man with bloodshot eyes and bad breath. The police thought that to be a highly specific description until they found it fit nearly everyone on the street that day. He got away and she is still the victim. She is still the victim not because of the physical wound she suffered, for it disappeared completely in four weeks, nor because of the financial loss incurred. But she, like thousands of others, was a victim because she played the role of the victim just as her attacker depended upon her to play it. She short-circuited through fear and was crippled by it at the time of the attack. She is still the victim because she allowed a social, emotional, and intellectual zero to scar her emotionally, probably for the rest of her life. Not only is she fearful of another attack, she has infected others with that same fear. Some pathetically ridiculous offender who has to hide in doorways or behind trees, lurking in alleyways or, figuratively, under rocks to sustain his miserable life, doesn't merit this reaction. She did the inexcusable when she reacted to his attack with fear because she responded just the way he hoped. He was looking for a frightened "mouse" and he found one.

The key factor in preventing this result lies in your mental attitude toward being attacked. Determine right now that you will not be the victim. Say to yourself, "Heaven help the poor guy who tries anything funny with me!" Take offense every time you are offended.

Controlled and properly channeled anger will afford you tremendous strength of courage, mind, and body. Anger blots out pain. Anger strengthens muscles and anger heightens mental alertness. Through anger you will be able to do things you never dreamed you could. Turn that anger against your attacker with immediate and explosive force. Unbalance him with your fury. He expects you to be frightened. He depends upon your being submissive. Don't play the game his way! Surprise him.

If everyone, as you will when you finish this book, would take offense every time offended, soon there would be no profit in offending. The tragic truth is that very few people take active offense to being offended. In fact, the situation has degenerated to such a low point that many people, even those offended outrageously, do not even report the offense to the police. Purse snatchers, obscene telephone callers, exhibitionists, sexual molesters, extortionists, rapists, and even burglars are permitted to go about their merry pursuits, unchecked, due to the lack of fortitude of their victims.

This nation is caught up in a psychosis of fear that is sweeping across it like a fever. People are afraid to walk in their own neighborhoods, even in the daylight. This is a national disgrace. This great big land of the "free and the brave" is rapidly losing its freedom because we aren't being very brave. Two percent of the national population is keeping the other 98 percent cowering behind double-locked doors, burglar-guarded windows, and electronically controlled fences. These human parasites, wastrels, and low-life jerks are making honest citizens afraid to speak to strangers for fear of being attacked. This is the only country in the Western world where the majority of its citizens live in fear of an unorganized criminal minority.

This country that was built by the superhuman courage and fortitude of its founders may be lost due to the timidity and faintheartedness of their heirs. The disgrace of this situation is not totally created by the criminality in this country, but also by the reaction to this criminality.

We must realize that whenever one person is offended in this country, everyone is offended. It isn't a crime against an individual but a crime against all of us. It will take a collective response of anger from all of us to stop the perpetrators. Once we stop playing the game the way the offender depends upon us to play it, then we will succeed in stopping his game altogether.

CHAPTER TWO

The Principle of the Weakest Point Adds Zest to Being Attacked!

What would you have done if you had been the lady in the story? Would you have screamed to attract the attention of the people on the street? Would you have kicked him in the shins and hit him in the head with your free hand? Perhaps you would have kneed him in the groin, as your father or brother probably instructed you. Maybe you would have screamed, scratched, kneed, punched, and kicked. Then again, maybe you would have done just as she did: short-circuit, so to speak, right down the middle of your very being. You may even have fainted upon his first touch of your arm.

Would you have screamed? Well, if you had, he would have been forced to shut you up. Your first little peep would have brought his hand smashing across your face in an effort to silence you. Even if he did not intend to hurt you, your screaming would trigger his automatic reaction of shutting your mouth. Don't get me wrong—screaming is a valuable tool in terms of self-defense, but it must be used at the proper time.

Would you have kicked him or perhaps given him the famous knee to the groin? You might think you would have, but he would

have jerked you off your feet before you came anywhere near your target. The first thing an attacker expects a woman to do is to kick or knee him, and he is set for either move. Yes, the groin is a vulnerable area, but most men have an instinctive reflex that protects them from being struck there successfully.

Maybe you would have slapped his face or tried to scratch his eyes out. If you had tried, more than likely you would have come no closer to his face than two or three inches before he countered your move. If he has control of your arm he has control of you. He can pull or push you, turn you sideways, or swing you against a lamppost. Then again, he could have been one of those peculiar types who enjoy all the kicking, punching, and flailing you can inflict, and he would stand there getting his fill before lifting your head off your shoulders by smashing your face with his fist. Generally, as soon as you make any move to strike him in such an inefficient manner, he doubles it back against you. Don't kick him, punch him, scratch, or scream as long as there is something else you can do.

A plan of self-defense must be mapped

out with your particular capabilities foremost in mind. This plan must be built upon the proposition that you cannot stand, toe to toe, and slug it out with your attacker (if you can, then give this book to a less capable friend). The most important strategy in your plan is your escape from your attacker. By immediate escape, you minimize the possibility of his injuring you.

The Principle of the Weakest Point Affords Escape

This is a marvelous self-defense principle that will facilitate your escape from almost any form of attack which your attacker might use against you. As a chain is no stronger than its weakest link, so the attacker's strength is no greater than his weakest point. The principle of the weakest point works like a miracle. By your turning all your strength, speed, and leverage against the attacker's weakest point of grip, in a surprise movement, you will break his grip instantly.

The attacker in the police report seized the young woman by the elbow and pushed her out of the line of pedestrian traffic, then held her in place by the strength of his grip. If the victim had used the principle of the "weakest point," it would have been impossible for her attacker to have held her in such a manner.

As surprising as it may sound, no man, regardless of how large or strong he might be, how good-looking or how homely he is, can hold on to you with his hands. No man can hold on to you with his hands because no man has as much strength in his thumb as you have in your entire body. The thumb is the weakest point of any grip held by the hand, but the thumb is three-quarters of the hand's manipulating ability. Try picking up a bologna sandwich without using your thumb and you will see what I mean. By turning all your strength and leverage against the strength of his thumb, you will escape the grip of his hand in a flash. Try to pit your strength against the strength of the fingers of even a weak person and you will fail to escape the grip.

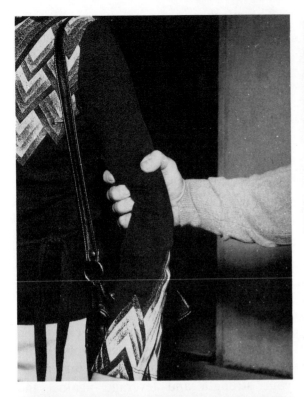

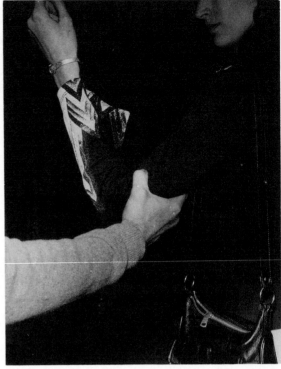

Let us illustrate the use of this principle by defending ourselves from a grip on the elbow as used against the frightened "mouse" in the police report. As soon as the attacker gripped her arm, she could have escaped. How?

By merely lifting her hand and forearm, then swinging it straight down behind his arm and hand. Notice in the illustration how the attacker's grip is dependent upon the control of his thumb in maintaining the hold on an elbow.

It is easy to cut his thumb away from the elbow by merely going over and behind it with your forearm. It is literally impossible for anyone to retain such a grip if you apply this self-defense principle.

Very simple move, but did you know it? The young woman in our story did not and chances are, if she had known the principle, she still would not have applied it. You have to determine that you will not be some parasite's victim and that you will make an effort to escape. Being so determined, you will be prepared to make a move. Making the right move is easy to learn, but making any move at all when caught by surprise is the difficult part of your defense.

Don't play the game he depends upon you to play. Dazzle him.

If you can force yourself to do anything, and you must, then you can break his grip easily.

Don't Just Stand There
Breaking the Grip . . . Escape!

As soon as you escape his grip then separate yourself from your attacker as fast as your legs will let you chug. Once separated by two or three quick steps (according to how excited you are, that may be ten to twenty yards), scream. What will you gain if you turn to face your attacker and slug it out with him? Even if you win, you are going to "bark" your knuckles and he isn't worth paying that price. Move away from him— but this is not letting him run you in fear. Move away from him because it is the smart thing to do. Let a little anger work for you and you will be amazed at how fast you can run and just how loudly you can scream!

Run toward other people. If you are on a deserted street, with no pedestrian traffic, go to someone's door. The people inside may be too frightened to answer but your attacker cannot count on that and he will probably flee the scene. If he does not play the game the way we want him to and he continues to come after you, then you will have to kill him. We will discuss this later. Most of the time you will be able to escape to some place of safety. However, don't get attacked until we cover this point. Let's continue exploring the principle of the weakest point.

The best way to utilize this book is to find yourself an "attacker." Rent one if possible—preferably by the hour. If this isn't practical, get together with a friend, or as a last resort, your husband or boyfriend. Unfortunately, the male ego makes husbands or boyfriends very poor practice partners. Once the element of surprise is removed from your defense, it is almost impossible to execute a specified technique successfully. Once your husband knows what you are going to do to break the wrist grip, for example, he will hold on to you to the point of having a hernia. It's an unusual fellow who will leave the element of surprise in his attack. However, if you have a fellow who will attack you as a stranger would and who will pretend he does not know what your defense will be, then you have yourself the ideal practice partner. You also have yourself a well-adjusted male companion.

In practice, have your partner attack you just as described, and then you respond as instructed. I will warn you when to be careful with your practice partner. Some of these techniques can be severely damaging and it is not practical for you to cripple your practice partner. Either you would have to wait for him to heal or you'd have to recruit another attacker. By doing some of these movements more slowly on your practice attacker than you would on your real attacker, the possibility of delays can be avoided.

You will find that defending yourself from attack is a fun physical activity. So much so, that you might want to invite a group of attackers and defenders in for a party. Group practice sessions really are a lot of fun.

When mastering these defense skills, try first to find the correct pattern of movement required in each technique, then increase the speed of the movement. Speed, timing, and leverage are three of the four principal ingredients of self-defense techniques. Without the proper blending of these elements in a smooth movement, the element of surprise, the fourth principle, will be lost

and your attacker will figure out what you are doing. Practice for speed of movement and the element of surprise will always be present unless you tell your attacker what you are going to do. Don't ever tell your attacker what you are going to do. Take it easy at first but work for speed.

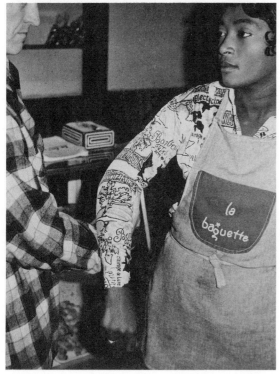

DEFENSE FROM ELBOW GRIPS

Elbow Grip #1: He is facing you and his right hand is on your right elbow.

DEFENSE: Bring your forearm up and over his thumb, then straighten your arm out behind his hand. You are free.

Elbow Grip #2: He is facing you with his hands on your elbows—holding, pushing, or pulling, it doesn't make any difference.

DEFENSE: Bring your forearms up and then roll them over his thumbs to a straight-arm position.

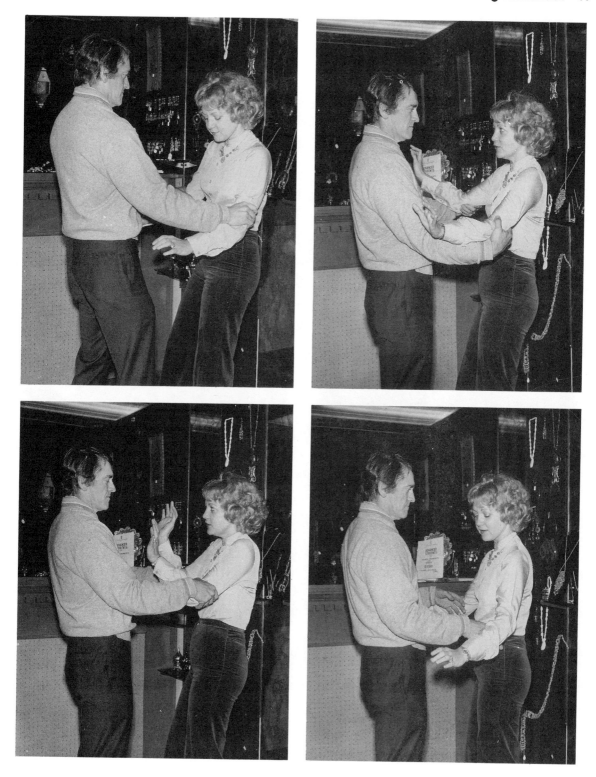

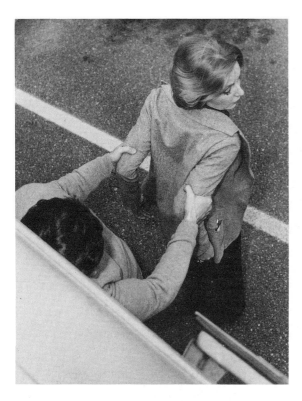

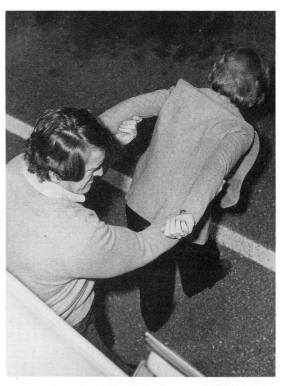

Elbow Grip #3: He is behind you with a grip around both elbows pulling your arms up behind you.

DEFENSE: This is actually the easiest escape so far. Merely follow the direction of his pull and let your hands come slightly together before rolling your forearms up in the direction of his pull. Roll over his thumbs and scoot away.

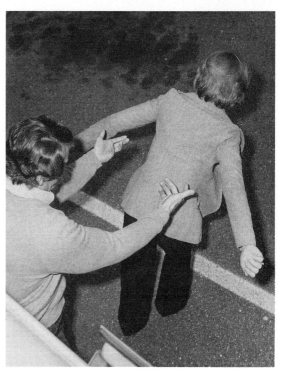

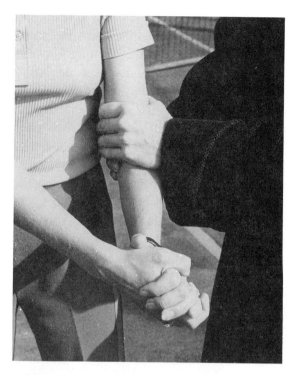 

Elbow Grip #4: He is standing beside you, gripping your elbow with two hands.

DEFENSE: This break employs a different weak point. Two-handed attacks on one limb call for the assistance of the free limb.

Shake hands with yourself, so to speak, and roll your forearm up and over, then forcefully behind, his hands. Do it slowly and notice how his wrists and hands are rotated. This wonderful phenomenon reduces the strength of his hands. We will use this principle against more dramatic forms of attack later in the book.

DEFENSE FROM WRIST GRIPS

The attacker seizes your wrist with one hand, pulling or pushing you or merely holding you in place. He could hurt you if he could maintain his grip, but he can't! When you apply the principle of the weakest point against his thumb, he can't hold you no matter how he might grip your wrists.

Wrist Grip #1: Left hand to right wrist—his thumb up.

DEFENSE: By going against his thumb with the sharp edge of your wrist in a leveraging movement, you are able to slip easily from his grasp. First, turn the sharp edge of your wrist to the opening between his thumb and finger. Even if he has a severely tight grip on your wrist, you will be able to make this turn due to the natural looseness of the skin on your wrist. Then lower your elbow to make a lever bar out of your forearm and move toward your attacker's grip. This move puts pressure on the side of his hand and pries his thumb open. Done with speed and surprise, you will escape him in the blink of an eye. Move away as fast as you can.

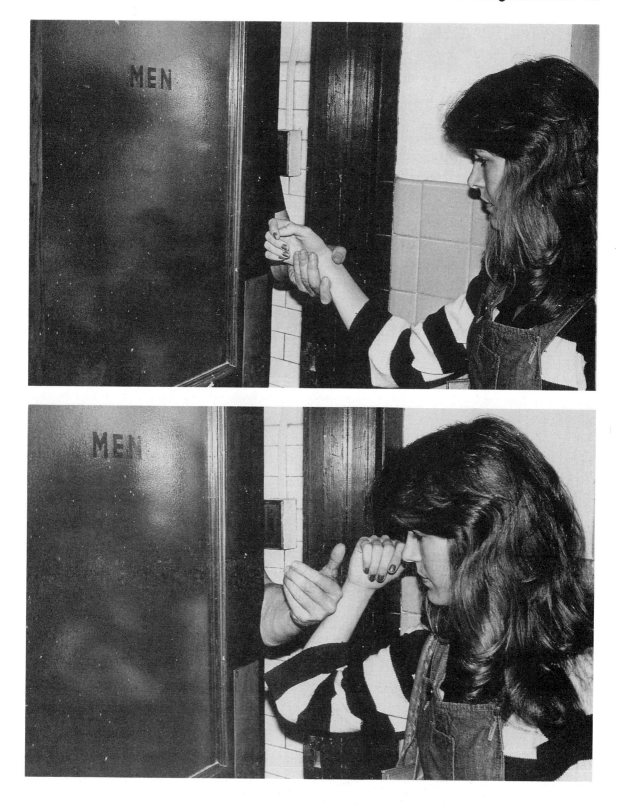

Wrist Grip #2: Facing you—his right hand to your left wrist and his left hand to your right wrist.

DEFENSE: Nothing to worry about. Same principle as above.

Merely turn both wrists to the opening between thumb and fingers, lower the elbows, and step toward your attacker.

You are gone.

Wrist Grip #3: His right hand grips your left wrist—his thumb is down.

DEFENSE: Remember the thumb!

You mean I have to look where his thumb is every time I am attacked? Yep!

Go against his thumb with all your force, straight up the side and behind the thumb. If he holds on too long—too bad. You break his thumb.

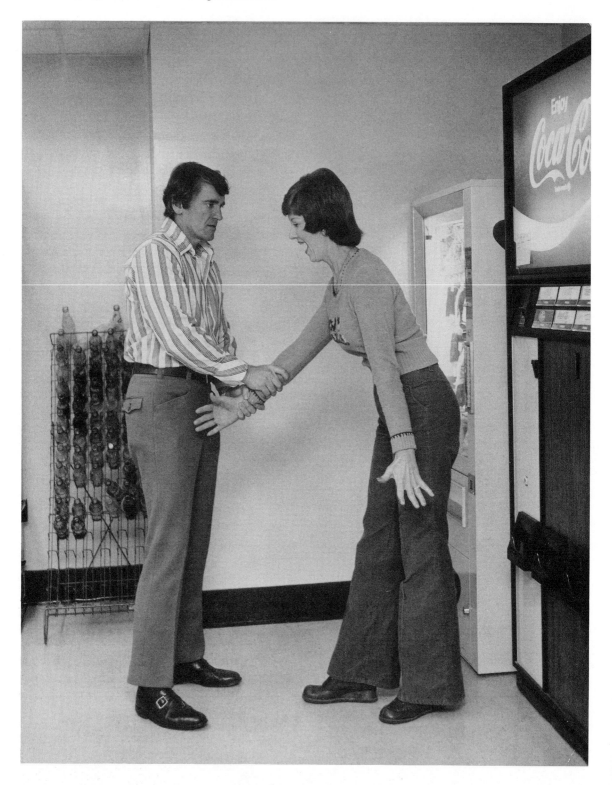

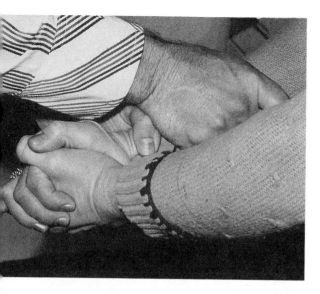

Wrist Grip #4: Two hands on one wrist.

DEFENSE: Oh, my goodness!

Don't worry, this is going to be fun. Shake hands with yourself as illustrated in the photograph.

Roll your hands up so that the sides of both hands are over his wrists.

Come straight down. Bang! That hurts—him, fortunately, not you.

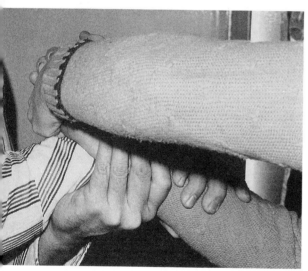

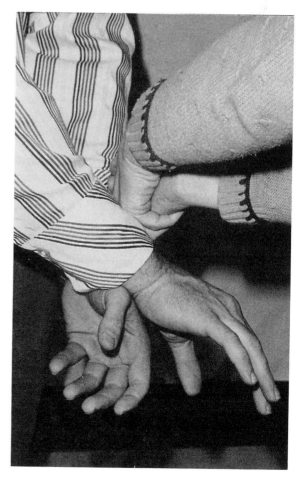

Wrist Grip #5: From behind, he grips both your wrists.

DEFENSE: This is tricky and has to be done just right. The element of surprise must be present in this defense probably more than in any illustrated so far. If your practice partner gets frisky and removes the element of surprise, then just take your foot and kick backward into his groin, simultaneously singing, "Surprise!" (Don't do that, I'm only kidding). Save that for strangers; they'll appreciate it more.

Let your little fingers lead the way. Roll your hands up and then crash down strongly on the outside of his grip.

This will cause his thumbs to pull to the outside, permitting you to escape.

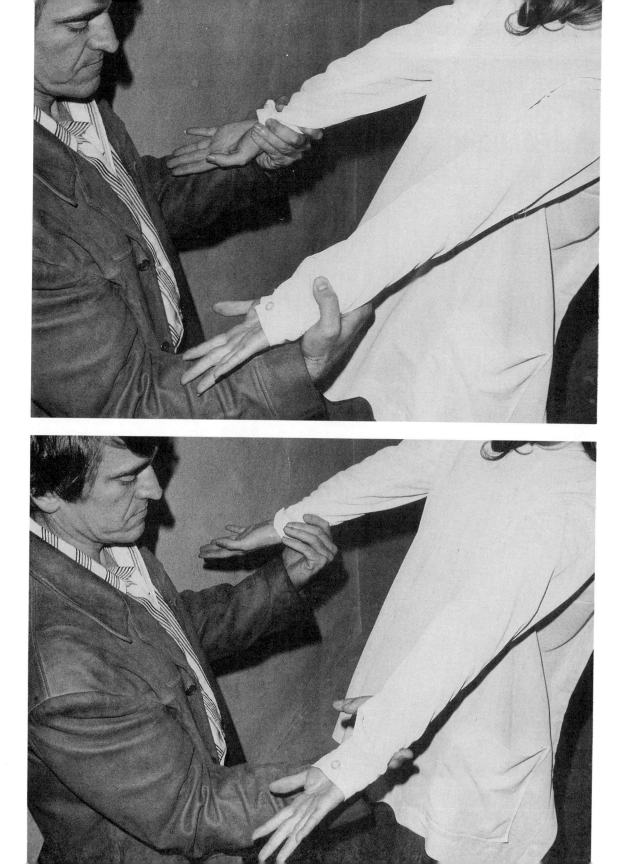

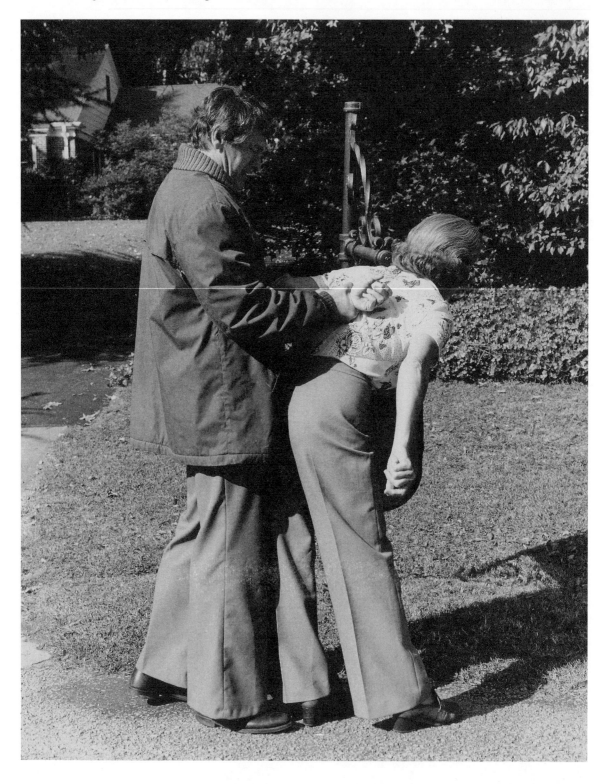

DEFENSE FROM HAMMERLOCK

One of the most common forms of attack is the hammerlock. Numerous women have complained that while they were growing up, their brothers used this grip against them.

This attack consists of two grips already discussed: an elbow grip, and a wrist grip. The defense is very simple: Yield to the force. Go in the direction that the attacker's grip is pushing you. Do not push backward against his strength.

Note the two grips—an elbow grip, a wrist grip.

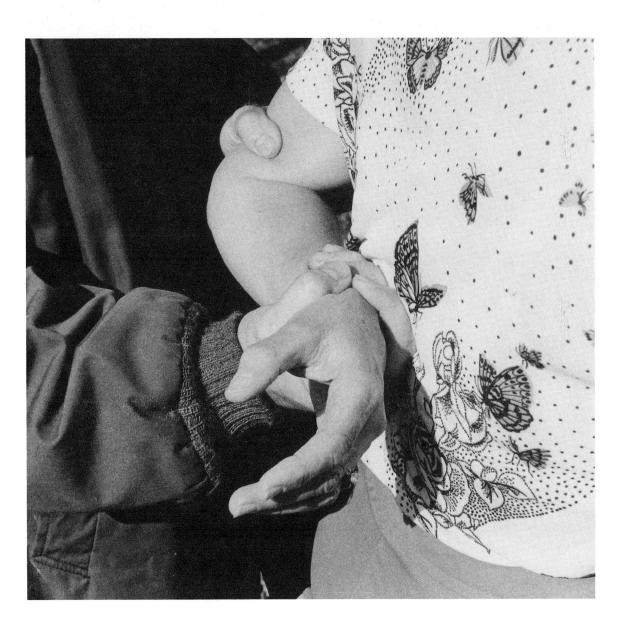

Lean forward to straighten your arm. This breaks his grip on your elbow.

As soon as your arm is straight, twist your wrist against his thumb. The faster you execute your forward lean and wrist twist, the greater will be his admiration for you.

DEFENSE FROM SHOULDER GRIPS

When the attacker seizes at the shoulder, he is dependent upon your wearing a coat of some sort. He does not seize the shoulder itself but, actually, the sleeve of the garment you are wearing. A raincoat, windbreaker, coat, sweatshirt, macintosh, wedding gown, or any garment made of heavy material can be used against you. When he seizes at the shoulder, as illustrated in the photograph, he has a lot of control over you. Yet, he has made a tremendous mistake. Now, not only can you escape, you can also break his wrist, dislocate his shoulder, or throw him on his back. If you don't get too excited, possibly you can do all these wonderful things at once.

How do you do all these wonderful things at once?

Shoulder Grip #1:   Standing beside you, he grips your left shoulder with his right hand.

DEFENSE: Straighten your arm and swing it forward, then backward, describing a complete circle. Don't stop. Continue your swing for another circle if possible.

When you circle your arm with speed, his grip is broken because his wrist is turned, which forces him to release his hold. If he is a real blockhead who holds on, you will break his wrist.

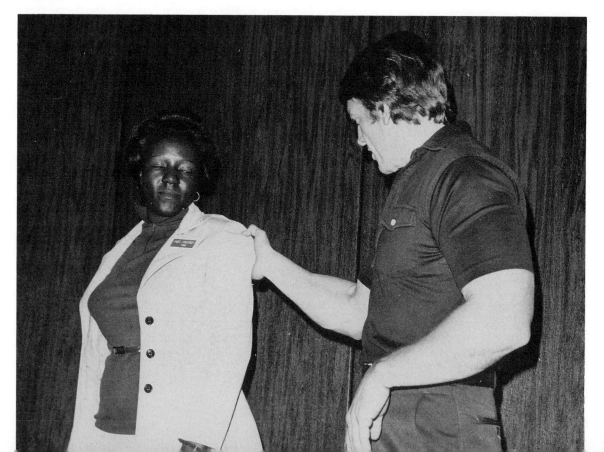

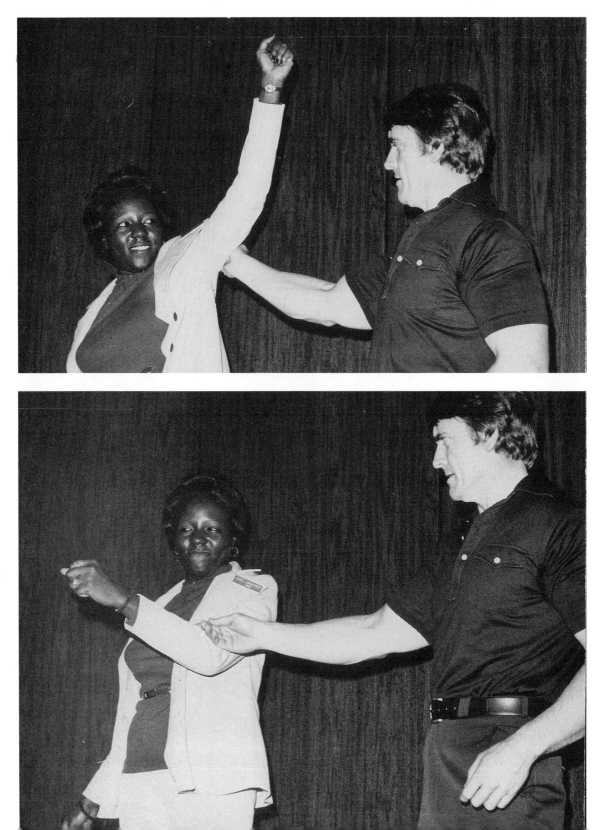

Shoulder Grip #2: Same grip and stance—
but this time he compounds his first mistake
by pulling you toward him.

DEFENSE: Warning! Do this at about half speed against your practice partner. Stop before making a full circle. Your practice partner is going to be miffed if you rip his arm out of its socket.

In this grip, the attacker's pull results in a bend of his arm as illustrated in the photograph. Circle your arm as before, but this time aim for that bent elbow. Hook the elbow and circle it around on your way up.

If it is a good day and you have used sufficient speed, you'll spin his arm in his shoulder socket. This is a terribly painful injury—which is terrific. If your speed has been a little slow or if he is light, he may just spin and only be thrown to the ground on his back.

Shoulder Grip #3: Facing you, he seizes your shoulders and pulls you to him.

DEFENSE: Same as above. Two hands doesn't change the defense. Just circle one of his arms and rip it right out of the shoulder socket. It doesn't matter which arm. If you circle the attacker's left arm with your right, turn your left shoulder away from him so you can get a couple of arm circles. Don't be greedy: You can only circle one arm. If you try to circle both arms, one will cancel the other.

As a parting gesture, you might want to put your heel in his ear. This is strictly optional, but if you are in a bad mood, kicking him in the head may serve to lift your spirits.

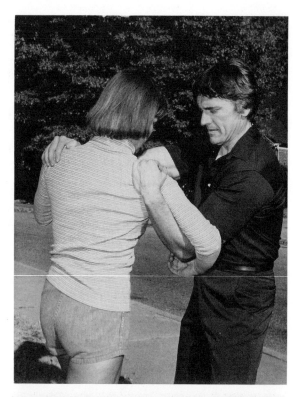

Shoulder Grip #4: Facing you, he seizes your shoulders and pushes backward with straight arms.

DEFENSE: Circle both arms between his and rotate your shoulders in his grip. This will break his hold.

Then push against his chest as hard as you can. Allow your push to send you backward.

You are not pushing him backward, you are propelling yourself backward and thus away from him.

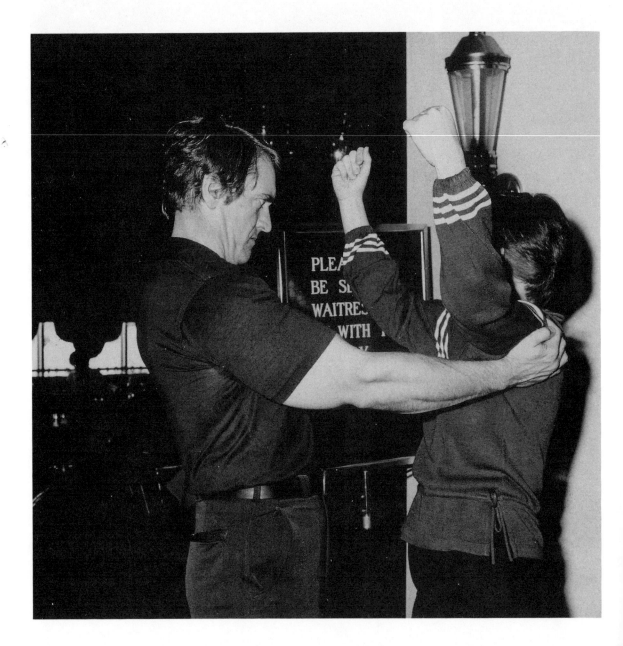

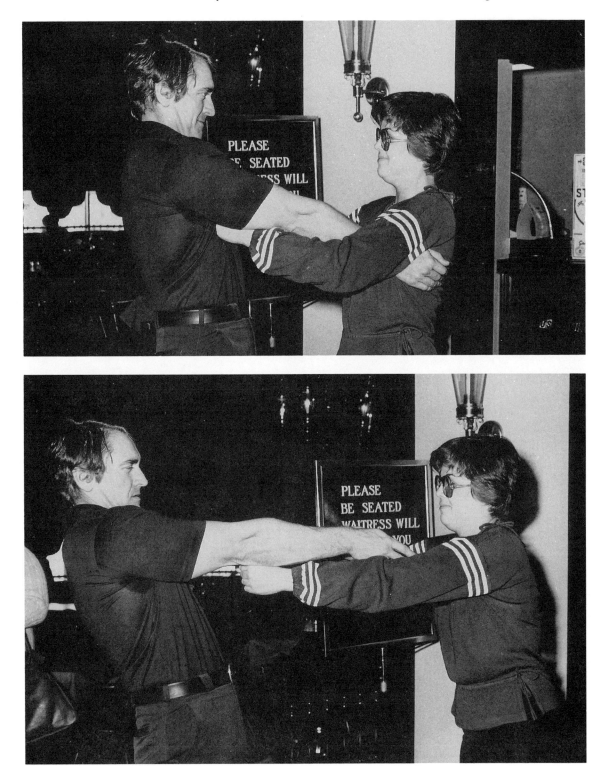

DEFENSE FROM CHOKES

So far, none of these attacks has been particularly dramatic. If your attacker seizes you at the elbow, wrist, or shoulder you have a moment to become something more to him than you were when he first seized you. Upon first contact, you are nothing more than an impersonal object that your attacker intends to work his will on, one way or another. But you have a moment to look into his eyes and appeal to his sensitive nature or introduce yourself, exchange telephone numbers or quote Bible verses to him.

Suppose you are walking, unaccompanied, across your favorite department store's parking lot or playing tennis with friends when an attacker from behind sneaks up and seizes your throat. Conversation is somewhat at a minimum at this point. In fact, you have about fifteen seconds, at the longest, to make your escape. The most typical reaction is to seize his hands and help him choke you. Even if you are very brave, don't try driving your elbow back into his solar plexus as so many self-defense instructors advise. If you do, you will make him angry and he will subtract seven and one half seconds from your allotted time. Use the principle of the weakest point.

Choke #1: From behind, he chokes with two hands.

DEFENSE: You must realize that as soon as you are hit, you are hurt. You must determine that you will not let anyone on earth make you his victim. If you can make any movement at all, you can easily escape a choke. You can move if you don't short-circuit.

By circling under his grip you are free.

To accomplish this, you curtsey and turn, sweeping your head beneath his hands.

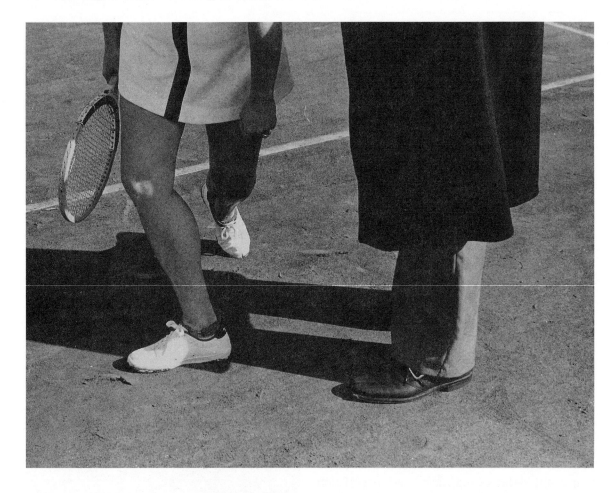

The key to this movement is in the curtsey. You can turn either way you wish as long as you are not being choked next to a wall. Extend one leg behind the other leg while bending at the waist. Follow the lead of that leg in a swooping continuing circle, which will cause his wrists to cross.

We have already seen what this does to the strength of his hands. You are free. (This movement will work anywhere except in small closets. Stay out of small closets with strangers!) You haven't escaped scot-free. Because you were hurt as soon as you were hit, you must go down the street screaming for two reasons—the first being to attract attention and the second being to open your throat, which he partially closed.

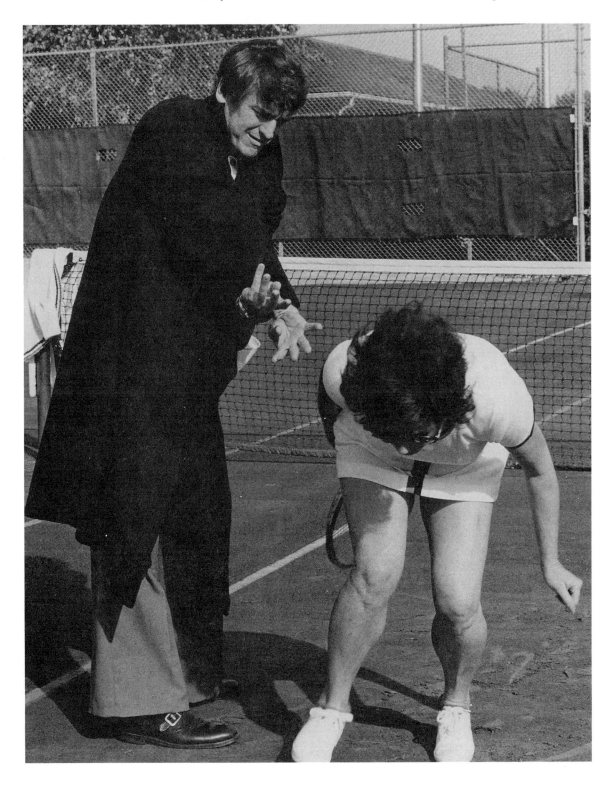

Choke #2: Front two-hand choke—his arms straight.

DEFENSE: This escape is called the "windmill break."

Thrust your left arm straight up as if attempting to strike it against your left ear. This action will either turn or trap your attacker's right hand.

At the same time your left arm is swinging up, you should be pivoting on your left foot.

The key to proper execution of this movement lies in your right leg sweeping in a circle behind your pivot leg and around to a position beside your attacker's right foot. This circling puts you well out of his grip.

The coordination of this movement is a little sophisticated and does take some practice. Take your time at first, finding the proper pattern of movement, then gradually work for speed. Thrusting your arm upward and pivoting on your foot is done simultaneously. If done with a sudden snap, and if your attacker's hand does not roll over when your arm comes up, you can break his wrist. However, if you have made your escape but realize you have not broken his wrist, don't go back to try it again.

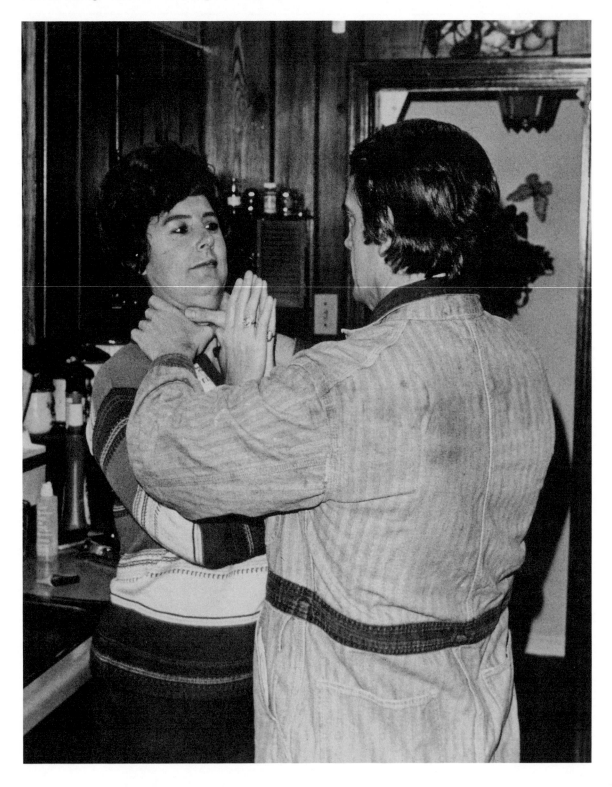

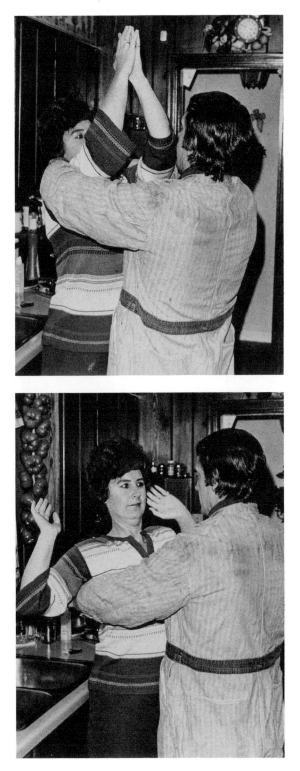

Choke #3: Front two-hand choke—attacker's elbows wide apart.

DEFENSE: This attack is typical of husbands and/or boyfriends. The attacker, in a blind rage, seizes you by the throat. His arms are bent and his face is close to yours as he shouts at you for being over budget, unfaithful, or whatever. This is called the "mad man choke." Bring your hands together in an attitude of prayer, then shoot your arms straight up and slightly back. Try not to let your arms contact his, because it is not the arms that make the break but the shoulders. Your shoulders rotating backward immediately break his grip. This is an amazingly easy technique to perform and it works like a charm as long as his arms are bent.

CHAPTER THREE

Unbalancing an Unbalanced Attacker Is a Delight!

Principles of Unbalancing

When I said you were going to look forward to being attacked I was thinking of your using unbalancing techniques against an attacker. Unbalancing techniques make being attacked an absolute delight.

Remember: Do not tell your attacker what you are going to do. So long as the element of surprise is present in your defense, it will work. Speed, timing, and leverage coupled with surprise make unbalancing your attacker easy and a heck of a lot of fun.

Upper Body Grip #1: The flirty guy approaches from the side.

You hesitate in front of your favorite department store to admire a dress on display in the window. You stand there trying to figure how to work it into your budget. Behind you stands a fellow admiring you and trying to figure how to work you into his budget.

He slithers up beside you and wraps his arm around your waist, offering to buy the dress for you. You might say, "Size seven" (or whatever) and encourage him to buy you the matching shoes and purse; but I hope

you would throw him to his back, leaving him screaming outside as you run inside—screaming, too.

Does that offending hand have to be at your waist for you to perform your throw? The truth is, if he knows anything about molesting, his hand is not likely to be at the waist. We know where it will probably be; but even if it is on top of your head, it won't make any difference. He's too close and that's his undoing.

DEFENSE: Take a little side step that places your foot behind and between his feet. Bend your knee against the back of his knee to break his balance while throwing your arm into his chest. He will go down with a bang and probably remain there in a crumpled heap. Off you go into the store screaming at the top of your voice.

It only takes a little pressure to send him sprawling, but since you have so much more to give—give your attacker all the force you can muster. If your favorite department store faces a street, watch him roll out into the traffic.

Bending your knee behind and into his, causing his knee to bend, is called "breaking the knee." Once the knee breaks, all strength is momentarily gone. Even if the attacker is six foot six and three hundred

pounds of muscle, his strength is all dissipated at the moment his knee breaks. At this split second, you can direct him downward in almost any direction desired. Isn't that wonderful? Of course you have to be quick, but it wouldn't be any fun if there were not some challenge to your efforts. Practice for speed.

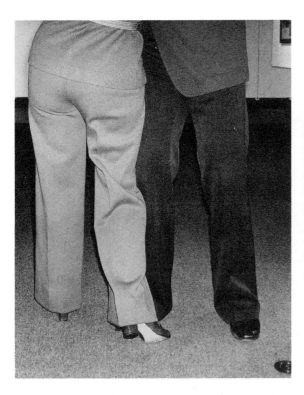

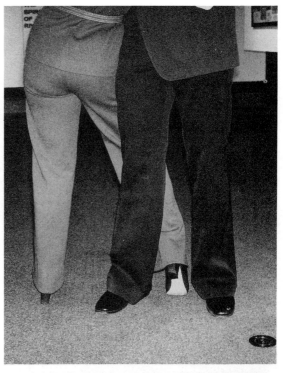

Upper Body Grip #2 Front hug—attacker's arms around your shoulders.

That impetuous devil hugs you to him with his arms around your shoulders and tries to nibble at your earlobes, or wherever. Don't take all that slobbering from a stranger.

DEFENSE: Swivel your hips out to the side, place your leg behind his, "break his knee," and lean forward.

Done with sufficient speed this is a powerful throw with devastating consequences.

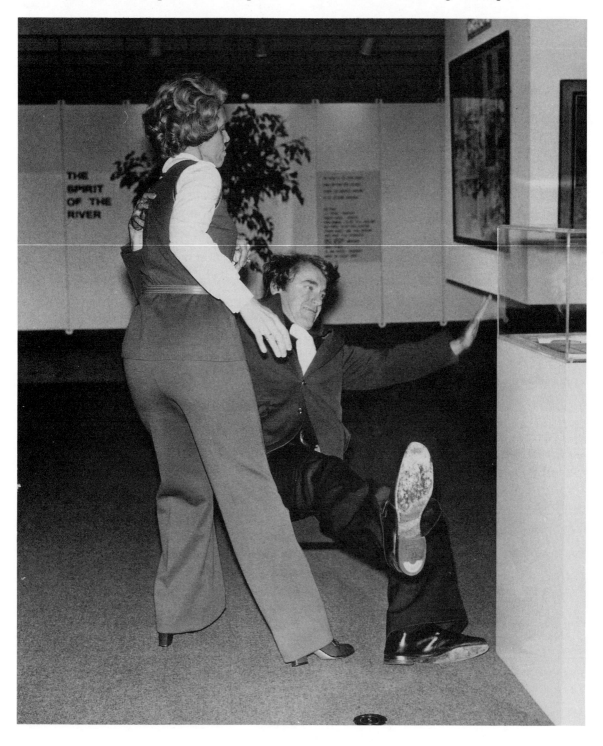

Upper Body Grip #3: Hug from behind—attacker's hands on your breasts.

DEFENSE: Warning! You might want to have your practice partner alter this grip somewhat; on the other hand you may not. You can get the same practice effect if he will wrap his arms around your shoulders. Occasionally his arms might slip up because he does not have the same anchoring advantage your real attacker will.

Women who have experienced this form of attack report that it is a real mind stealer. It needn't be. In fact it should be a lot of fun. A lot of fun because it affords you one of the most powerful unbalancing possibilities offered in this book.

Swivel the hips out to the side, then step behind his leg and lean backward.

Done properly, you'll lift him off his feet. The first thing to hit will be the back of his head. Will he hold on? Not likely, because it is a natural instinct to throw the hands back to cushion the fall.

Upper Body Grip #4: Front bear hug with your arms free.

DEFENSE: He just wants to love you a little with this attack. This is a great way to be attacked unless you are a person who finds it difficult to make decisions. This form of attack affords nearly all the vulnerable area strikes detailed in Chapter Four as well as a great unbalancing technique. Because he has left you with your arms free, you may choose to kill him, maim him for life, or just bounce him off the back of his head. Few attacks in life present such wonderful possibilities.

Unbalancing techniques are truthfully more fun than vulnerable area strikes; so unleash this powerful move on him: Place one hand under his chin and your other arm behind his back (low but not too low, as you do not want him to become emotionally involved).

With your hand on his back, pull him snugly against you while driving his chin straight up with your other hand. The initial push on the chin is not backward, as one might assume: It is straight up. This tips his head backward and, as the knee break does, instantly unbalances him. Pull on his back and follow the arc created by your driving his chin upward.

Lean over him but don't attempt to hold him up; just let him go and watch him bounce.

Upper Body Grip #5: Hug from behind— his arms around your waist, leaving your arms free.

DEFENSE: This is a "breathtaking" form of attack. Generally when anyone is seized in this manner all breathing ceases until escape is accomplished. In this position, he can limit your breathing until loss of consciousness occurs. However, for the length of time it will take you to break this hold you won't need to breathe anyway.

It is easier to perform this unbalancing technique if you distract your attacker a little. He has left your hands free, so strike back for his eyes. It is a great plus factor if you hit his eyes but it really doesn't matter if you miss. You are merely thrusting for his eyes in an effort to distract him from your main target, which is his foot.

You don't even have to pick up his big old cloddish foot. Just hold on to it a moment because as you bend down to seize it, your bottom goes backward, causing him to take a backward step. Hold on to that foot and he is going nowhere but down.

This unbalancing technique is accomplished through a very sophisticated form of leverage. You sit down and back into his leg rather than merely bending downward and seizing his foot.

Many times the throw can be accomplished without seizing his foot. Sit on his leg and press backward with your seat. Grasp his ankle and pull it up as you stand erect again. This holding of his ankle serves to balance you forward as well as assuring his going down.

What would you do if he pulled you down on top of him? Well, you know where you are going because you initiated that direction. Sit on his stomach! Put your bottom into his stomach with as much force as you can generate. It will knock the breath out of him this time. Then with as much ladylike dignity as you can muster, simply roll your leg over and off you go down the street. Don't forget to scream.

Upper Body Grip #6: Mugger's choke.

DEFENSE: The mugger's choke is named after the good old happy guy who chooses to attack a woman in this manner. The mugger sneaks up from behind, rings you around the neck, and pulls you backward to a doorway, automobile, or alley, behind a tree, into the rectory, or wherever. He is looking for a sincere, meaningful, and lasting relationship. He plans to spend a little time with you. Go with him. Don't pull away. You've been looking forward to this moment!

Don't have a tug-of-war with him, pulling against him with your neck as the "rope" in the middle. Go in the direction of his pull.

Turn his strength against him. As soon as he wraps his arm around your neck, nestle your head against his shoulder. Yield to his force completely. By doing so you destroy his force. Seize the arm he has around your neck to determine which way you must direct your break. If it is his right arm then you must turn to your right and vice versa.

As he pulls you backward, flow with him and keep up with his step. When you have his timing down, turn in the direction he is pulling you. If he is a right-handed attacker (three-quarters of all attackers are right-handed) . . .

. . . simply let your right leg swing in a wide circle as you make your turn.

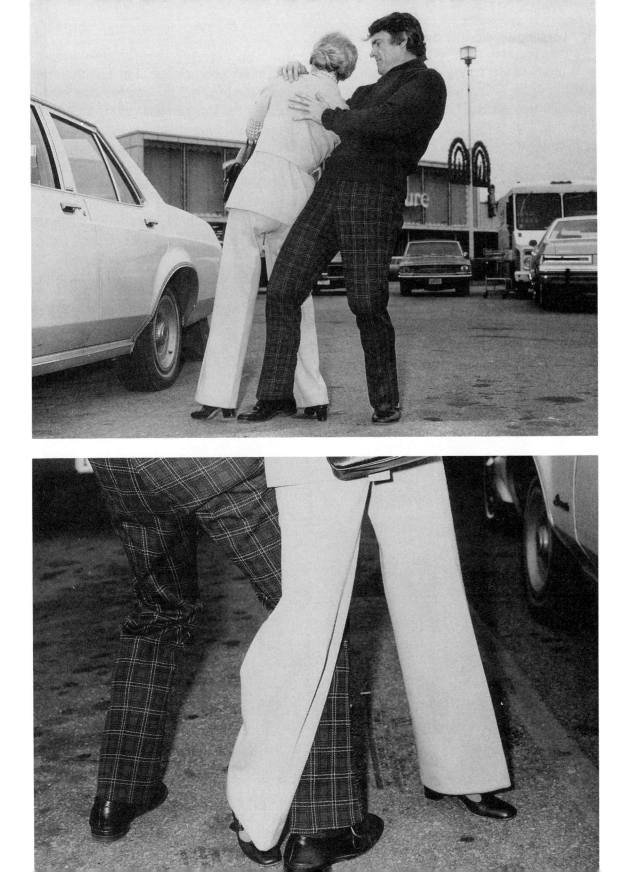

When you are facing the direction of his pull, your right leg will be directly behind his right leg. He will automatically trip over your leg.

Put a little something extra into your defense and pull him over your right leg. Don't panic and you can do this movement without any trouble. The harder and faster he pulls the easier he makes it for you.

Every other time you've been instructed to run down the street screaming after you have made your escape, but not this time. This is the big one; the number one form of attack in the United States. This time linger on the scene long enough to tippy toe up and down on his head two or three times, then run off down the street screaming and laughing at the top of your voice. Would you please call the police; they would like to know how the silly clown got there like that with all those funny heel marks on his forehead.

Upper Body Grip #7: Mugger's choke without the pull.

DEFENSE: The attack is almost identical to the more typical mugger's choke but this time he is not as interested in you. He is just fooling around waiting for the green to clear. If he is mugging with his right arm then he will probably be amusing himself on your body with his left hand. Don't let the roaming left hand distract you.

Seize his right arm, and take a step directly to your left with your left foot.

Swing him forward and around over your right leg. If you do this movement fast, you will cause both of his feet to leave the ground. If you are playing in a foursome, everyone will admire your follow-through.

CHAPTER FOUR

Life Affords Few Pleasures That Can Equal the Striking of Vulnerable Areas!

There are five main vulnerable areas of the male body (four for the female body). Each one is a joy in itself. These vulnerable areas can be poked, squeezed, clapped, kicked, scratched, punctured, slashed, stomped, slapped, lacerated, spindled, folded, mutilated. To do all of these for one attack would be terribly bad taste, of course.

The order of vulnerability is as follows: (1) the trachea; (2) the ears; (3) the eyes; (4) the solar plexus; (5) the male groin. Never strike for any other area when vulnerable area number one, the trachea, is open. If he is wearing a tie or clerical collar, then you will have to choose a second vulnerable area. If he is wearing earmuffs and a thick woolly scarf around his neck, you are limited to just three vulnerable areas. If you are attacked by a scuba diver you are in trouble.

Attack #1: Two-hand choke from the side.

DEFENSE: I would think that even if it was your dentist who had you in this grip, you would be a little excited. With that excitement will come a little adrenaline, which will give you the possibility of at least one hundred and fifty pounds striking force. This is very fortunate as there is no principle of the weakest point break for this particular form of attack. You are going to have to turn your strength against his in the most efficient manner. What part of that male anatomy are you going to strike to do the most damage?

You're right! The trachea!

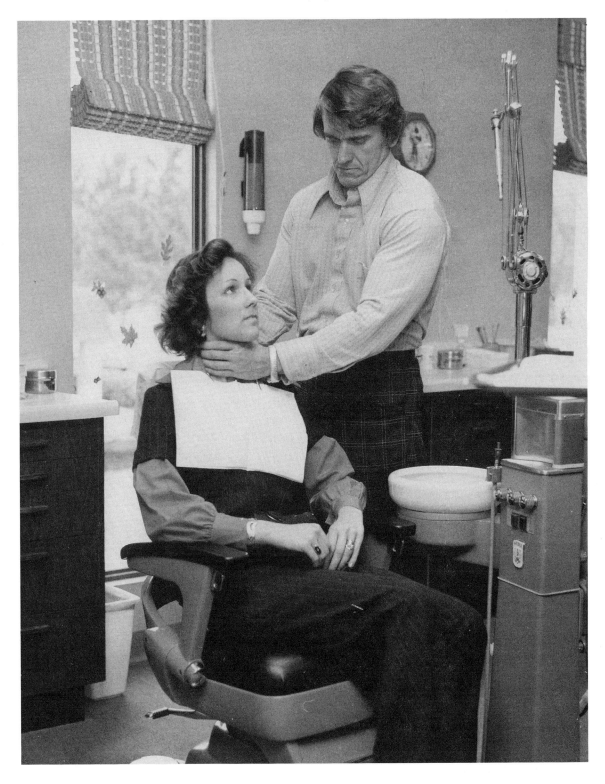

For this defense, look at the small hollow area in his neck just above the sternum and drive your stiffened fingers straight through it. Strike so hard that your fingers will figuratively pimple out the back of his neck. If done properly, everything in between is going to be crushed. If the attack takes place on the street corner, run down the street because it is a gruesome sight to watch someone die in this manner.

You couldn't strike someone like this? Sure you can; you are taking his life before he takes yours!

Remember this vulnerable area because you will be using it on several more occasions. In fact, whenever in doubt about what to do . . . close his throat! Of course, you have to be judicious in the use of this technique. If someone walks up to you and asks for directions to get out of town, you can't panic and close his throat; that's not polite and, besides, it's against the law. In addition, it is embarrassing to attempt a tracheotomy in public without the proper tools.

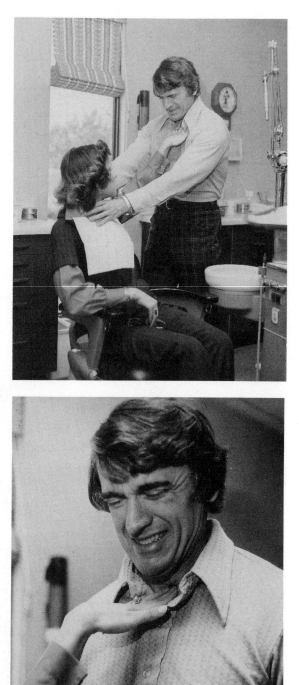

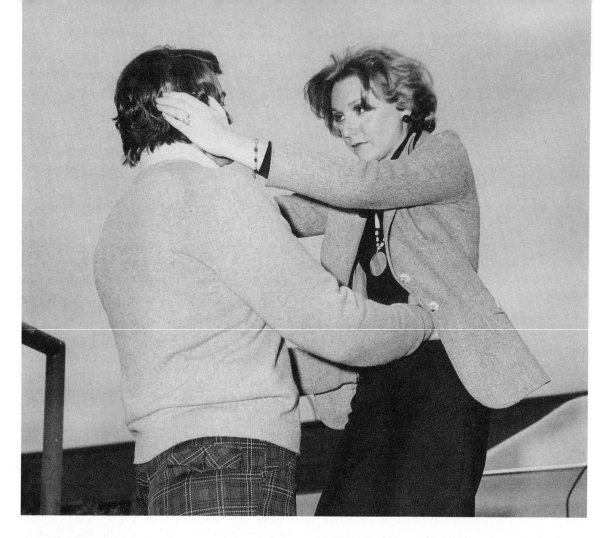

DEFENSE: There is that look in his eye which immediately reveals his intentions. He reaches out for you. Stop him before he gets started.

Applaud the first part of his performance. Clap him on the ears. Bring those hands from your back pockets and slap him squarely on both ears. If he hears anything at all, it will be like a bomb going off in his brain. More than likely he will not hear a thing. Nine out of ten times you will render your attacker unconscious. There is a 20 percent chance you will kill him with this strike, so think twice before using it on husbands. This strike will work like a mira-

cle every time as long as your attacker is not deaf. Bad luck if you are attacked by a deaf attacker. Doubly bad luck if you are attacked by a deaf priest.

If, in the above attack, the attacker had been more successful and had wrapped his arms around your waist with "steel band" strength, attempting to squeeze life's breath from your body, you might have inquired, "Hey?" If he had answered, "Huh?," then you would have known he had hearing. At that point, you could have looked up into his big smoldering eyes and then smashed your hands, open-palmed, against his ears. You would have had him falling at your feet.

Attack #3: Bear hug from behind—your arms are pinned against your body.

DEFENSE: This is another bone-crushing grip. This time, he has you in a position that affords you very little movement. There is no swiveling of the hips that would allow you to break his knee and you can't take his eyes out because your hands are bound at your sides.

What can you do? This chapter is on vulnerable areas, isn't it? So . . . raise one leg to clear the area, then seize and squeeze! I'll bet he will let go. In your excitement, don't forget to let go. Don't pull him down the street behind you. (Warning! Slapping your practice partner's thigh will be sufficient. If you can hit his thigh, then you will be able to hit the actual target if the real situation presents itself.)

If he lifts you off your feet in this attack, just bend your knees and run-in-place, so to speak; the target is the same vulnerable area. Drive your heels into his groin for as long as he cares to hold you up to do so. At the same time, if you can get things coordinated, you can drive the back of your head into his face. It won't hurt your head in the least because the skull is the hardest area of the anatomy and has very few nerve centers. Use your head as a battering ram whenever the opportunity presents itself. Witnesses to the attack will even compliment you by yelling, "That's using your head!"

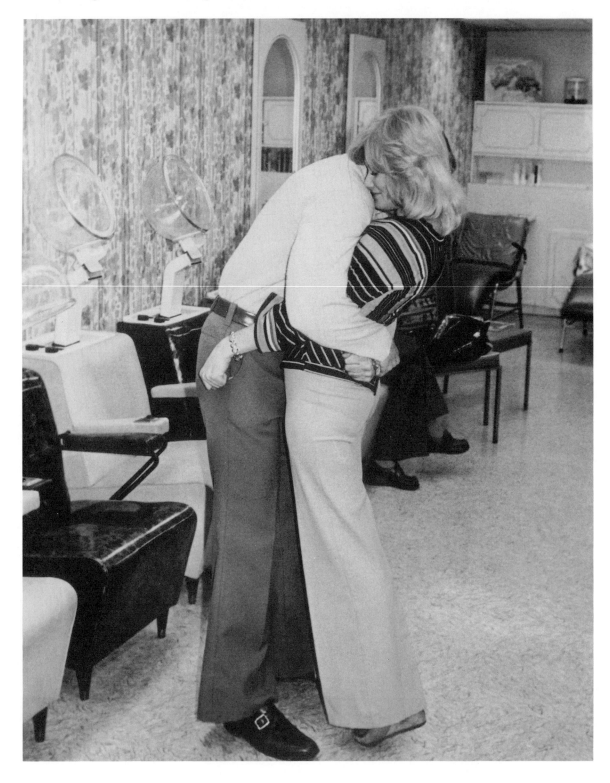

Attack #4: Front bear hug—your arms pinned against your body.

DEFENSE: Here is the reverse of the above situation. If your practice partner is your husband or boyfriend, here is an opportunity to make an interesting experiment. Have him seize you in this bear hug. His arms should be wrapped around your arms and he should be squeezing you tightly against him. Don't let him have any idea what your defense is going to be.

Brace your thumbs as illustrated. Press your thumbs into the soft area of his abdomen as demonstrated in the photograph. All males have a reflex action to jump backward when this technique is properly executed. If he does not at least move his hips backward as soon as he is jabbed, start looking for a new husband or boyfriend. The reaction you are looking for is a sudden jump backward, which may or may not be accompanied by a release of the arms. In the hundreds of times I have demonstrated this in police-recruit classes, I have never had a male fail to respond with the desired reaction. Three-quarters of the time, I have had to ask the "attacker" to repeat his attack but not let go completely in order for me to demonstrate the full technique. Forty percent of all the women who have "attacked" me in this manner have had the same reaction.

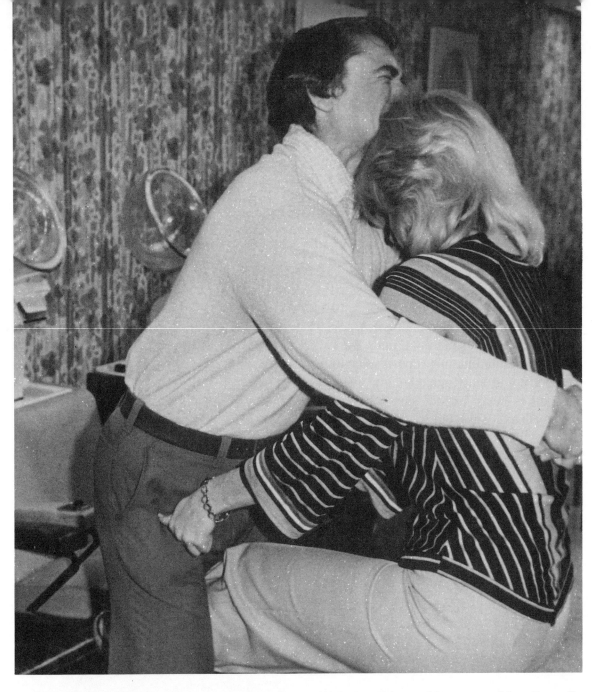

The complete movement is a touch in the area illustrated accompanied by a backward step, which separates you from your attacker, and a drive with your leg up into his groin. Whatever strikes him is just fine. You never know how touchy your attacker is going to be, so you can't predict whether you will knee, shin, ankle, or toe him. It really doesn't make any difference as long as you kick him good and hard. Don't be gauche and stay around to gloat. Run down the street screaming; maybe he will save face to some degree anyway.

Attack #5: Two-hand choke from front—crisscross break.

DEFENSE: The attacker's arms can be straight or bent in this choking attack. The break is called the crisscross strike.

With the open palm of your right hand cross over to strike the wrist of his choking right hand.

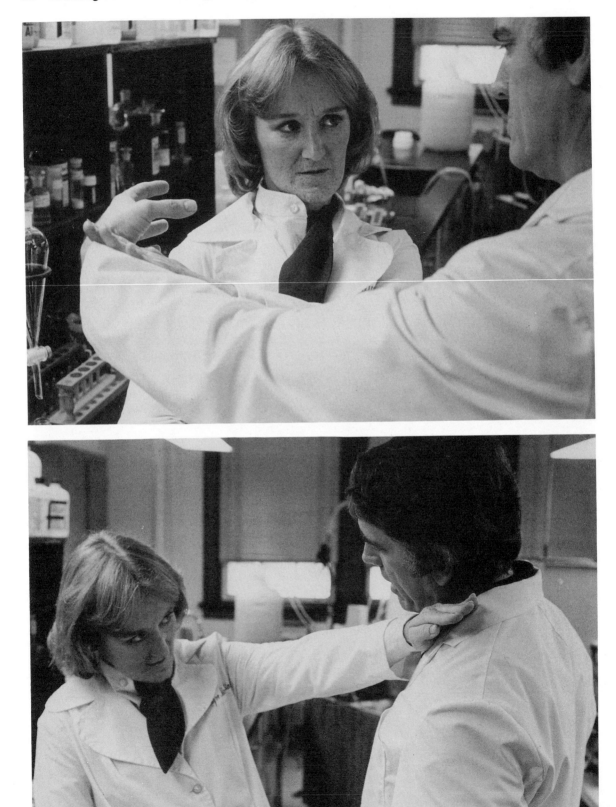

Then immediately cross over with your left hand and strike the wrist of his left hand. This is not a push but a thrusting, striking blow to the wrist. Don't travel through with the strike. Hit the wrist then carry through only about four inches. Striking his wrist in this manner causes the hand to release at the point of contact.

Just as soon as the left hand's grip has been broken, bring the knife edge of your left hand cutting back across his throat. This is generally not a killing blow but will produce disabling choking spasms in the windpipe of your attacker. If the carotid artery is sufficiently crunched it will render him unconscious. Spasmodic or unconscious, it is all the same to you. You have escaped.

Life-Threatening Attacks

Every form of attack detailed so far has eventuated with your escaping relatively unharmed. In the following attacks, as soon as you are hit, you are hurt. You have to be 100 percent on top of this form of attack or you will be six feet under. This is a life and death situation—your life opposed to his death. This time your attacker has caused you limiting injury. You cannot escape immediately, so you will have to kill him. Well, we don't want to be all day about it.

You might have a hair appointment or a dinner date or maybe you are late for work, so you want to do it in the most efficient manner. Incidentally, you may scream now because you have already paid your price. He has hurt you, so scream because it will help you withstand the pain and scream because it will give you strength for what you have to do.

Killing him can be done with your fingertips, but it is really more efficiently done with one of those weapons you conceal about your person every day: a ball-point pen, nail file, rattail comb, car keys, toothbrush, or possibly a hand ax (a hand ax, dagger, or sword is a more efficient weapon than a ball-point pen, but if you walk around town with a hand ax, dagger, or sword in your hand, you'll never be attacked).

"What am I doing with a ball-point pen in my hand when I'm being attacked? Writing a get-well card? Taking a test?" You're right. You have to have the ball-point pen in your hand, as you can't politely ask him to wait until you get it out of your purse. So whenever and wherever you are uneasy or a little anxious about walking, have this fantastic weapon in your hand. You won't offend anyone by carrying a ball-point pen in your hand regardless of where you might be. Fortunately, your attacker probably won't even notice that you have the pen. If he does see it, he won't worry about it.

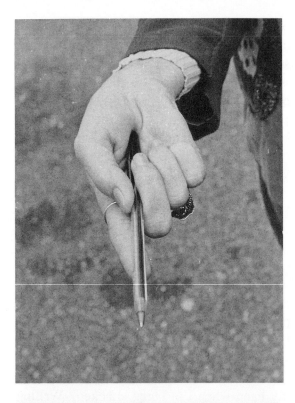

Brace the dull end of the pen against the heel of your hand. Let your index finger extend down the length of the pen just short of the point. Push the tip of your finger against the side of the pen to force the other end of the pen firmly against your palm. Use that same index finger to lead the way in your thrust with the pen. You literally point the way to your target. Look at your target and point; you'll never miss.

What is the target? There are two: (1) the throat; (2) the eyes. Nothing else will work at this point.

The Throat: Drive the pen into the trachea so far that it comes out the back. Purposely, consciously, separate the vertebrae on your way through. If you don't kill him, you will leave him paralyzed for the rest of his life, and in this case that is terrific.

If he is wearing a tie, then hook that pen into the side of his throat and let it come out the other side. He will drown and choke to death in his own blood.

Or, drive that pen straight up under his chin in the fleshy area between the jaw-bones. Let it be just like hooking a fish, and when he opens his mouth to scream you'll be able to read the name of the manufacturer and the price!

The Eye: If his head is down covering his neck, then drive that pen so deep into his eye that you wouldn't be able to pull it out. Of course, you wouldn't want to anyway; in fact, if there is any left, give it another push.

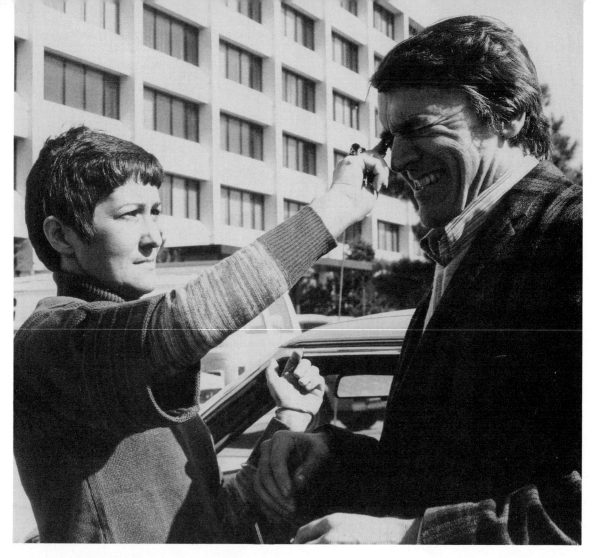

Another fantastic weapon likely to be handy is a key. Have your car keys out whenever you go to or from your car. It's an efficient thing to do. It is also a time saver that might be a life saver because if he grabs at you and you can't escape, you can always backhand him across his eyes. Rip across his eyes with the saw tooth ridges of the key. Don't use a forehand strike because that is too easy for him to block; backhand him across his eyes.

One day while discussing this use of the keys, a woman asked me, "What about his nose?" I said, "Lady, do you mean put that car key up his nose? You're sicker than I am." "No," she said, "I mean that if you strike across his eyes, you'll hit one but will be thrown off the other by the bridge of his nose." I replied. "Don't be so greedy; one eye is fine, but if you are worried about this, just follow over the bridge of his nose then dip into the other eye!"

Gross, right? Unfortunately, it is necessary for you to have this callous attitude. You must determine that you will not hesitate a moment to do what is necessary to protect your life. Don't let anyone make you his victim!

Applying Pressure Against Joints to Surprise, Bewilder, and Gain the Admiration of Your Attacker!

As I have said, you are subject to attack anywhere you are in today's society. So there you are seated in church (temple, synagogue, mosque) and the dirty old man seated beside you places his hand on your thigh. If you happen to have a ball-point pen handy, you can drive it through the top of his hand; but be careful not to stake his hand to your leg! Fortunately, there are many more pleasant ways of defending yourself from such attacks.

USING PRESSURE AGAINST JOINTS

Offensive Gesture #1: Sitting beside you, he places his hand on your thigh.

DEFENSE: You place your right hand on top of his hand and at the same time place your left hand under his elbow. Press down with your right hand and roll his elbow forward with your left hand.

Drive his elbow so far forward that it upends him, leaving him counting the pieces of chewing gum stuck beneath his seat. Pat him on the "popo" and find yourself another seat.

If you are seated in a theater, which is more the proper setting for such an attack, his head might strike the seat immediately in front of him. This is fine. If you are myopic, which causes you to select a seat in the front row, then you will roll him head first, flat on his back, below the screen. This is fine, too.

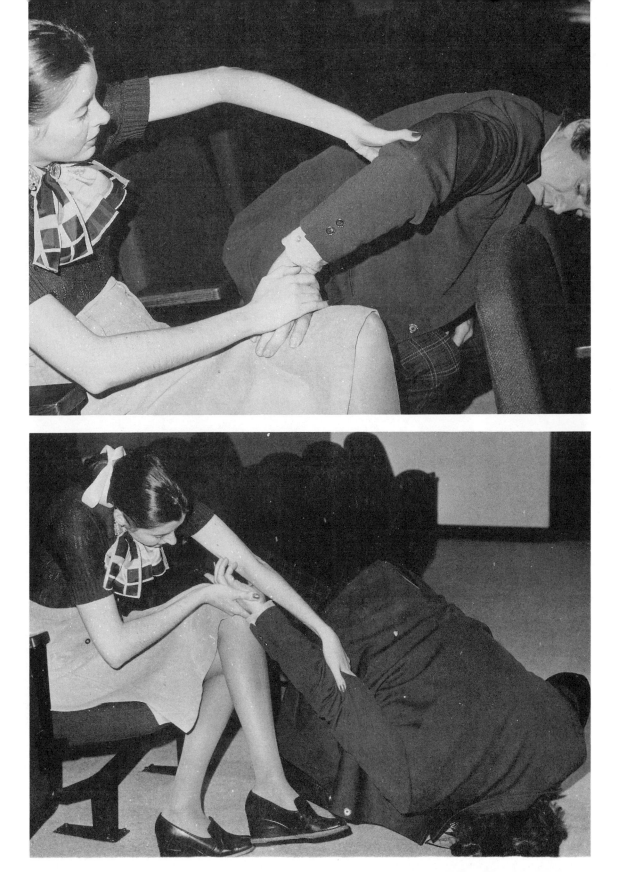

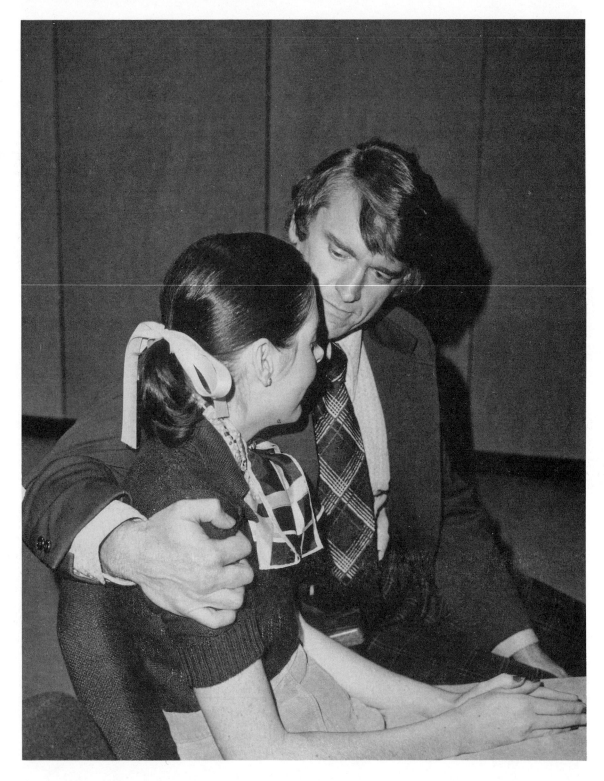

Offensive Gesture #2: Sitting beside you, he places his arm around your shoulders.

DEFENSE: With his right arm around your shoulders, he squeezes your shoulder in a flirtatious manner.

With your right hand, play with his fingers as if you are returning the flirtation.

Seek a good grip on one of his fingers, preferably his little finger or the ring finger, then rotate out of the seat as illustrated.

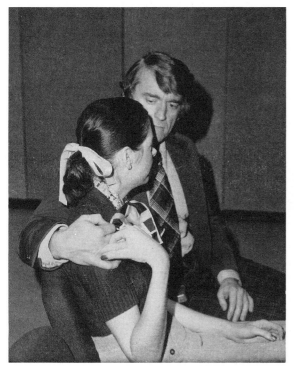

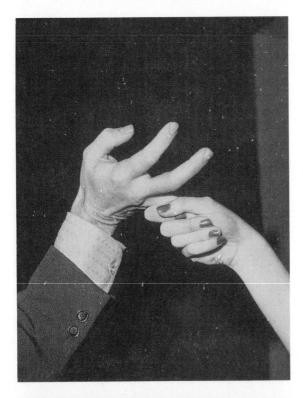

Pull his hand toward you, and at the same time push backward on the lower part of the finger that you are controlling.

Take him to the manager. Make him sing the national anthem. Make him do anything you want because he is at your mercy. If you break his finger, don't let go. Even if it feels "sickypoo," carry him to a place where you will be safe before you release him.

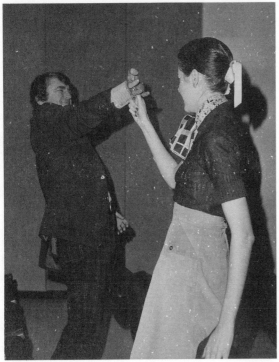

Offensive Gesture #3: He stands in front of you being offensive.

DEFENSE: You have endured three hours of the longest party of your life. To make the situation worse, for two and a half hours a stranger has stared at you from across the room. Finally, he walks over and strokes your earlobes. He has an earlobe fetish. Nothing could be more offensive than having your earlobes stroked at a dull party.

Place one foot behind his ankle and the other foot on his knee. Hold him in place with your foot behind his ankle and push back with your foot on his knee. This exhibition will make the two of you the hit of the party.

Any time you are seated and an attacker is standing close enough for him to hit you, it will be possible for you to drop him using this ankle-block, knee-push technique. Practice the movement with your legs crossed.

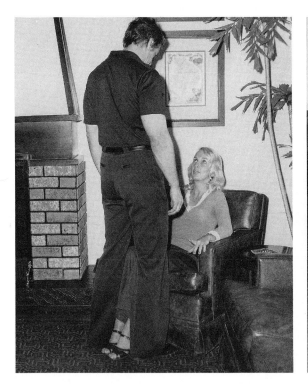

It is also possible to do this technique by using both feet against his knees. If he straddles your knees as in the photo, then bring both feet up to his knees. Curve your feet around his knees, pulling toward you to break his stance, then push diagonally out and backward. He looks so ridiculous just before he falls that this technique is cuter than the other.

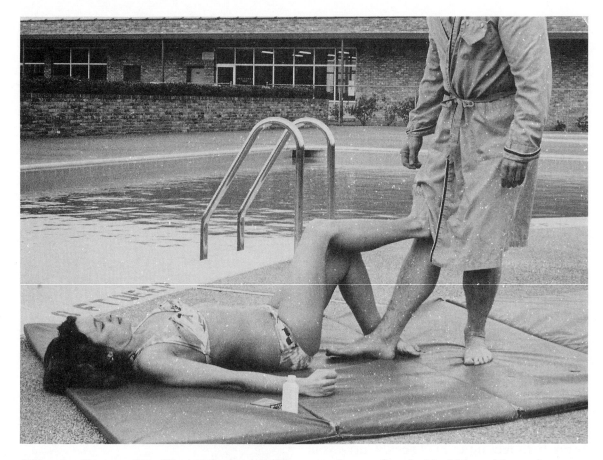

Offensive Gesture #4: He stands at your feet while you are on your back.

You are sunbathing on the beach and he walks up to look you over. He is blocking your sun.

DEFENSE: Vacationing on the beach is too expensive to allow anyone to block your sun, so place a foot behind his ankle and one on his knee.

Hold and push to drop him on his duff.

This defense is also practical if your attacker knocks you down. Just before he follows you down, block his ankle and drive his knee away from you. Any direction you push the knee, more than likely, will work for you.

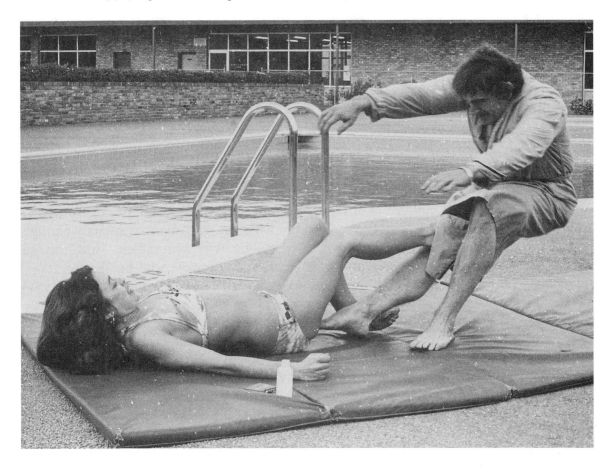

CHAPTER SIX

Putting the Old Spark Back In Your Obscene Telephone Calls!

There are millions upon millions of obscene telephone calls made annually in the continental United States (I don't know about Hawaii or Alaska; I would speculate that there are many made in Alaska but very few in Hawaii). Don't feel ego-threatened or despondent if you have not received an obscene telephone call. Look forward to that moment because it is probably just a matter of a few weeks before you hear those classic phrases over your own telephone.

Some obscene telephone callers are true artists. I am afraid, however, that most people who try their hand at the art lack the necessary verbal acuity to ever become great. Many people who realize their inadequacy for the undertaking merely breathe heavily into the phone. The counter here is to offer the breather soft words of encouragement. Don't hang up; keep him breathing for you and very soon he will hyperventilate, then pass out.

There are so many young children ranging in age from six to thirteen trying to make obscene telephone calls that the art has degenerated to a pitiable state. Children lack the maturity for such an undertaking. Phrases built around words such as "wee wee" and "poo poo" lose their shock value.

It is becoming increasingly difficult for even the true artist to use original obscenities when the mass media constantly barrage the public with obscenities. How can he continue to compete with the theater, movies, magazines, gag T-shirts, and TV specials? The pressure must at times become unbearable.

At self-defense demonstrations during the past six years I have asked women if they have received obscene telephone calls. In every group, the majority have said they have received at least one such call. However, in the last year I have had some women say they thought they had but were not really sure! I can understand this dilemma. It is becoming increasingly difficult to determine where public entertainment leaves off and offending obscenities begin.

Despite the confusion, there are still hundreds of women who find the obscene telephone call an agonizing experience. Typically, the lady at home answers the phone, "Hello . . . would you mind repeating that?"

He does, verbatim, and in shocked confusion she slams down the receiver. The phone rings again in fifteen seconds. She answers this time with an entirely different attitude. She picks up the phone with trembling hands and perspiring palms to barely whisper,

"Hello." He greets her with the same opening line. With a little whimper of pain, she again slams the phone onto its cradle. Well, if you play it this way he will fall in love with you! You'll be on his calling list for a very long time to come. He will call you in the morning, after lunch and, worst of all, he will call you at two A.M. (The most obscene telephone calls are those made after midnight. It's not so much what they say, it's just the fact they are calling so late.) The whole purpose of the obscene telephone call is to get a shocked response. The typical reaction is to play the game just the way the caller expects. Don't do that, and that's no fun; and obscene telephone calls have to be a lot of fun.

If you called the police to report your first obscene call, you probably found them to be little more than sympathetic. They were sympathetic because that is good public relations. If you have reported one to the telephone company lately, you probably found them indifferent to your complaint. There are so many complaints of this nature that neither agency can do much about your first three or four obscene calls. To get help, you must endure a number of calls so that a pattern can be established in order to get a fix on the caller's line. Don't listen to all that garbage for weeks; handle the calls on your own.

When you receive your next call from an obscene stranger (don't do this to obscene friends; you'll offend them), say to yourself, "Hot dog, at last an obscene call!!!" Pick up the whistle you have placed beside your phone for this purpose and blow into the transmitter as hard as you can, then slam the receiver down. Depend upon his calling you

back because he will probably be another slow learner and will call you back using his last good ear. Well, blast that one too!

If he calls you back a third time then you have a real "Lulu" on the line. This time use a little more strategy: Before you blast his ear, giggle just a little bit. This giggle lets him understand you are beginning to enjoy the game the two of you are playing and you are looking forward to shattering his eardrum every time he cares to dial your number.

At a demonstration where this advice was given, a woman popped up out of the audience and declared, "I did that and I loved it!" You could tell she really had loved it. Then as an afterthought hit her she added: "He called me back thirty minutes later and blew a whistle in *my* ear." Apparently after that exchange of pierced eardrums, she never heard from him again.

If you are receiving more obscene telephone calls lately, but seem to be enjoying them less, you may want to put the old spark back into those precious moments with Super Sound. Super Sound, a fascinating little gadget, makes obscene telephone calls a delight. Keep it beside your telephone if you can.

If at last you get an obscene telephone call but find your husband, roommate, or darn kid has moved the Super Sound, don't lose your opportunity as it may be three weeks before you get your next obscene call. Hold on to that moment. Say: "I am sincerely interested in every word you have to say. I wouldn't want to miss a word of this but you have caught me in the shower. I am standing here in a puddle of water and I have goose bumps all over my body. If you will give me a moment to get a towel, I will be right back. Now, don't go away." Lay the phone to the side and rush through your house to find the Super Sound. Dash back to the phone and say, "Are you still there? Oh, good. What's that you were saying? . . . Oh, yes." Now point Super Sound toward the transmitter and let him have a long blast. The effect is devastating. Count ten and then say, "You sure have a way with words." You will have to wait at least ten counts or he will not be able to hear you.

Not nearly as much fun as the above but possibly your best bet is to merely depress the button on the phone. Your obscene caller lives for a response. That response could be a slammed phone. His fantasies lift him into ecstasy when he hears a combination of gasp and the phone slammed back onto the carriage. Don't give him anything. When you depress the button before you return the receiver to the carriage, he experiences a total physiological cutoff. He has received nothing. He may call back a few times to see if it was a fluke. Just depress the button each time. He will give up on you to seek more rewarding numbers.

A lady in Illinois told me that she had been receiving an obscene telephone call from the same person off and on for five years. There was no established pattern to his calling. One afternoon she was hurriedly ironing a formal for her teenage daughter to wear to prom night. The phone rang and it was the obscene caller. She said, "Look, I . am too busy right now to talk to you. Just give me your number and I will call you back." And he did! She took the number automatically and suddenly realized, "That's his number!" She called the police and they arrested him at his home fifteen minutes after his call to her. What a wonderful surprise for everyone.

CHAPTER SEVEN

Is It Ever Possible For You and Your Burglar to Have a Meaningful Relationship?

A Brief Profile of the Average Burglar

By nature, burglars are shy and skittish individuals tending to be withdrawn and antisocial. They much prefer to be left alone in your house with plenty of time to rummage through your possessions, weighing the value of each article. They tend to be night people with a distaste for light and airy surroundings. Most burglars are not disposed to hard work entailing prolonged effort but much prefer the simpler challenges of standard locks and casement windows. Though quiet, they are not particularly neat. Some burglars leave houses in shambles. I'm afraid the majority of burglars detest animals of any type and have marked antipathy for barking dogs. Some burglars have experienced near heart attacks after stepping on sleeping cats in darkened rooms. Definitely on the plus side: All burglars have a keen sense of hearing with a special attunement for their surroundings. They can hear cars in the driveway, keys in the lock, conversations of next-door neighbors visiting in the yard, and you inside your house. Because burglars are so retiring, it is extremely unlikely that he, she, or they will enter if you are heard within your home.

You Are Inside and He Is Outside

You are retiring for the evening (or if you want to make the situation a little more difficult, you can say the children are tucked away in another bedroom down the hall), when all of a sudden you hear the rustling of leaves, and the cracking of acorns, and you see silhouetted against your shade someone outside your window. How do you handle that person outside your window?

Scream at the top of your voice, "I know you are out there. I've got a gun, and if you don't get off my property I'll shoot you. I have just called the police!"

You haven't called the police and you may not have a gun, but he sure won't know the difference. And 99.6 percent of the time a burglar hearing such a lie will practically break his neck fleeing. A cat meowing is enough to make the average burglar break into a panicked run. Let him know that you are at home and you don't welcome his intrusion.

If you have any doubt that he has heard you, pick up a lamp and throw it through the window, pick up a drawer and throw it through the window, pick up anything you can get your hands on and throw it through the window. Make sure he has heard you.

What if it turns out to be the 0.4 percent of the time? What if he continues to enter after you have raised all that ruckus? At this point, you can legally assume in any state in the fifty that he is coming to kill you. If he comes in the front door, then you go out the back door. If that is not possible, but you happen to be lucky enough to have a shotgun handy, then take aim and blow him in two. If both halves fall outside, run outside to pick up one half and throw it inside. However, if both halves seem too heavy, or if it has been raining and you've just had your hair done, then call the police and they will throw one half inside for you as a public service.

Seriously, if you have given the poor unsuspecting burglar warning that you are at home then you can take a cannon and blow him into the next county (or parish) and not one fragment of his person will have to land on your property. The two legal requirements here are (1) he must be entering and (2) you must give him a warning. Well now, that certainly seems fair, doesn't it? Someone who has chosen to burglarize your residence instead of all the other houses in your neighborhood deserves some recognition. Don't blow his head off until you let him know that you care.

If you don't have a shotgun then call the police and wait for them to get there. Agree? Certainly call the police, but don't wait for them to get there before you take some self-defensive action. You could be "ground-beefed" and packaged by the time the police arrive. The average response time for the police across the nation is three minutes, but on a busy night it might take them forty-five minutes to answer your call.

If you can't escape, or if you won't escape because your children are in the house, then rush to the kitchen and secure a knife which you use to cut up chicken or whatever. Stand in a corner with your hands behind your back. Play "which hand is it" with your burglar. If he comes toward you, let him get close, fake with one hand, and surprise him with the other. Get his attention with the empty hand and then drive the knife deep into his throat with the other hand. It will be a mess all right, but unavoidable under the circumstances. Don't let anyone make you his victim!

At a self-defense demonstration given to a group of senior Americans, an elderly lady shared an experience she had had with a would-be burglar. She said that for the last twenty years she had lived by herself in a large two-story house fronting a well-traveled street. One morning, around 2:00 A.M., she was awakened by a banging on her front door downstairs. She sprang out of bed and dashed to the head of the stairs in time to see a large bulky man push through her front door. She said that when he hesitated and looked up, she realized he was not Santa Claus. In an inspiration, she turned toward one of the empty bedrooms along the hall and called, "Harry, get your gun, someone has broken in!" Then she looked to another room and shouted, "Paul, get up. Frank, come quick."

She said the man immediately turned and ran out the door, closing it "with such a clatter!"

You can handle the situation because you are so much smarter than your burglar that the two of you live in different worlds. Bluff him—don't let him bluff you. Remain calm.

Let him take the property if he remains calm enough to do so, but don't let him mess around with the owner.

He Is Inside and You Are Outside

In the middle of the day, you drive onto your driveway with a carload of groceries. You lug a couple of sacks to the door and discover it unlocked. You are certain you locked it when you left for the store. Would you feel too silly to go next door and call the police to have them come to check your house? Most people have felt that way.

The typical reaction in this situation is to disregard the certainty of having locked the door and to enter despite the eerie feeling accompanying such an action.

You walk through the living room, pass into the dining room, and you suddenly become aware of a noise in your kitchen. You stop short. The noise in the kitchen ceases and you can almost hear the person listening for you. After a frozen eternity, a stranger appears in your kitchen doorway (not a particularly good-looking stranger at that) and the two of you stand eyeing each other. Finally, it is you who musters the courage to ask, "What are you doing here?"

He musters enough courage to reply, "I'm taking everything in this house I can carry." Your reaction? "Hey, can I help you? Find you a box? Fix you a cup of coffee? Give you a lift with the TV?"

Don't do anything to stand in his way at this moment. Don't scream because you will cause him to panic and he may stampede all over you. Remain calm (don't be overly solicitous, he may become interested in you and forget what his purpose is), let him take what he wants and leave. It will be a reflex action for him to escape immediately without taking anything with him. However, if he is one of the truly cool ones who does happen to want your TV, then do get on one end of it and help him carry it to his truck.

It is a very foolish game to attempt to defend property. At this moment, much more is at stake. Remain calm. You have encountered a very excited and potentially dangerous person. Don't cut off his avenue of escape. If he cares to take something (other than you) with him as he leaves, consider yourself very fortunate.

If he shows interest in you, then let him get close but then kill him. Vulnerable areas numbers one and three are your best targets at this point. Close his throat or take his eyes out. Remember, don't attack him. Let him escape if he will. However, if it's hurting you he has in mind, kill him. Don't let anyone spoil three minutes of your day; no one has that right.

If you return to your residence to find a door is unlocked which you know was locked, or a window opened when it was closed, don't assume your burglar has left. Leave as quickly and as quietly as possible. Go to the nearest phone to call the police. Tell the operator there is a burglar inside your house. He may not actually be there but police respond to the call faster if they think a burglar is present. They get more credit for catching a burglar than for merely taking a burglary report. You can understand the difference in enthusiasm, I am sure.

It is amazing how many people automatically dash inside when they find the front door ajar. They erroneously assume the burglar has finished the job. What a surprise it is to discover he has not!

Let the police look around for you. Not only do they get paid for doing this, they actually enjoy it. They especially relish the task if there is a strong possibility of the burglar's being actively engaged in his merry pursuits. In addition, even if the burglar has fled the scene it is a lot easier for the police to reconstruct the crime if you have not rummaged through the evidence before they arrive.

Discouraging the Burglar

Daylight burglaries are on the increase. Paradoxically, although easier to be seen, the burglar is not as likely to be noticed. A person approaching a neighbor's door late at night might draw your attention, but consider your reaction to someone driving up to your neighbor's house in the middle of the day evidencing a natural businesslike manner. Would you take notice? Most people do not. Burglars disguised as yard men, salesmen, delivery boys, repairmen, exterminators, bill collectors, and marriage counsellors wander through neighborhoods at will.

Remember, burglars prefer to be alone. Leave your radio on while you are away. If a burglar tries your door and hears the radio, he will be less prone to venture any farther even if your doorbell is unanswered when he tries it. He knows that there are people who, while at home, will not answer the doorbell for one reason or another.

Barking dogs are a deterrent. Big monstrous dogs that throw their bodies against the door when the doorbell is rung will keep everyone from your door—friend and foe.

Even small dogs with tiny ear-piercing yelps will discourage the burglar. It isn't the bite in the dog, it is the bark in the neighborhood which irritates the burglar.

A second automobile parked in the drive serves as a deterrent to the burglar who hasn't done his homework well. The presence of the automobile presents the possibility of someone being home.

Window guards, open fences (ones which block entrances but not view), well-lighted areas, homes close together, people at home during the day, and nosey neighbors are all great burglar deterrents.

Happiness to a burglar is newspapers on the porch day after day, a light burning in the window day and night, grass growing uncontrolled in the yard for weeks, high shrubbery in front of windows, conventional locks, neighborhoods without pets (except for goldfish—burglars don't mind goldfish), high "keep the world out" fences, and, happiest of all, cold unfriendly neighbors who wouldn't give the time of day to anyone.

There are few professional burglars, and most part-time burglars need more than casual encouragement to break into your home. To provide this, you need to keep large sums of money in your home and make a point to discuss this fact with your friends in public places. Make a public display of your enthusiasm for your new stereo equipment or rare book collection.

Although anyone can be burglarized, it is an unfortunate truth that the majority of victims set themselves up for the burglary. Don't play the burglar's game. There is no way to keep a burglar out if he is determined to enter your house, but don't make it easy for him. Most burglars are lazy louts who despise making prolonged, exhausting efforts which consume precious time. If he breaks your window and turns your window latch but finds the window will not raise because you have the window blocked with a broomstick handle or nail, he will go next door hoping your neighbor has not been so enterprising. If he springs your front door latch only to discover a deadbolt lock still facing him, he will call it quits and go home for lunch.

Watch your neighbor's house and have him watch yours. If you see a stranger seated in an automobile parked on the street, ask if you can assist with address or directions. Letting this person know he has been noticed will deter him from taking action. If he has legitimate business, he will not be offended in the least.

Make the undertaking of breaking into your house too chancy for your burglar. If you want to go as far as the burglar alarm system, that's okay if you have the extra money. To me, such an investment is like being victimized in reverse. The burglar has cost you either way you look at it. Little precautions will work just as well. Don't be victimized by anyone. Make *them* pay the price. Invest a little thought, but don't invest a lot of money.

CHAPTER EIGHT

Don't Shoot the Peeping Tom; He May Be Your Next-Door Neighbor!

Prowlers are not burglars. Prowlers may become burglars if given half a chance. But prowlers are not burglars until they burgle.

Whereas burglars are generally undereducated, dullish louts, prowlers may turn out to be fascinating folk if you can slow them down long enough to get acquainted.

Prowlers are almost exclusively night people. Just like their less colorful cousin, the burglar, they hate dogs, lights, nosey neighbors and, especially, drawn draperies or shades. They also find damp grass a real nuisance. They, like the burglars, love high shrubbery in front of the windows but loathe the sticky leaf variety. Occupational hazards for prowlers are the shrubs with little points on each leaf. Prowlers can be identified by the ever-present scratches on wrists and ankles. Prowlers generally have a much better knowledge of your neighborhood than the burglar. They should, because they are usually your neighbor.

Prowlers can belong in any age category but prowling is mainly an avocation of the young. Both sexes prowl but prowlers are predominantly boys.

There seems to be a biological urge in boys twelve to fifteen years of age to prowl around the houses in the neighborhood. Most prowlers are peeping toms. They are almost exclusively harmless unless cornered. When cornered, some kinky accountant who lives in your neighborhood may fight to the death to escape discovery of his identity. Frighten the prowler away but don't attempt to capture him.

Sex is generally the motivation in peeping tomism but it is also a flirtation with danger, sort of a harmless (?) nighttime adventure practiced by young teenage boys. Don't shoot the prowler with or without warning. You don't have a legal right to execute people crossing your property.

I'm not condoning peeping tomism nor defending people who peep in your windows, but if every peeping tom who has peeped under a shade had been shot, we would probably be missing a few presidents today. Burglary is a felony. It is a very dangerous act if the burglar mistakenly enters an occupied dwelling. Peeping in windows or prowling property is a misdemeanor. It is a nuisance act.

Although far less legal danger is involved as a threat for the prowler, he usually moves much faster than the burglar when discovered. Both move like the wind but, as explained before, the prowler usually knows his territory better than the burglar and is able to traverse the terrain with much surer steps. Let the prowler know you know he is there. You don't even have to learn a new set of lines. Use the same monologue for the prowler as you did for the burglar; it will work just as well. Actually, most people identified as would-be burglars probably were no more than peeping toms in the first place. Neighborhoods are crawling with peeping toms.

At a recent demonstration, a woman shared with her group that she and her family (consisting of two teenage girls) were plagued with prowlers one summer. They suspected the young boy who lived three doors down the street. However, one morning's check of the grounds proved their suspicions misplaced. Beneath her younger daughter's bedroom window, the lady discovered a cigar. It was a very unusual brand of cigar. She carried the half-smoked cigar to the banker who lived behind them and presented it to him in front of his wife saying, "Here is the cigar you dropped at my daughter's window last night. You must be more careful where you throw these. Littering is against the law."

Some prowlers may not be prowlers, but actually city service employees on legitimate business. During years as a police officer, I have been required to pass through hundreds of backyards in the middle of the night. Telephone linemen must on occasion cross yards to get to poles. Electric company service people are on duty around the clock and have occasion to cross properties in order to check faulty equipment. Don't shoot the prowler; it takes time and money to train efficient service people. If you hear someone outside your window, demand he identify himself. If his mission is not legiti-

mate, he will be off faster than you will ever be able to get a description of him.

The prowler has been treated rather lightly here but he should be reported every time to the police. Report every offense. Take offense every time offended. Keep the police in your neighborhood informed as to what is going on; they want to feel needed. Help them help you and you will reap fantastic dividends.

Your Prowler Chooses to Linger Awhile

Three A.M., and you are awakened from a sound sleep and looking into the eyes of a stranger. Not a very good-looking stranger at that. It is obvious he is not interested in your property. Don't scream or make any movement at all, other than your natural inclination to shake. Let him get close, comfortable so to speak, and take his eyes out. To thrust the thumbs into the eyes is like nothing more than sticking your thumbs into a well-congealed bowl of jelly.

Do it in the most effective and efficient manner. Go a little beneath the eyes with the thumbs placed on the lower rim. Then push your thumbs in. Tight little sockets that they have, the eyes will go straight out! They will not roll across your bedroom floor. They are connected to sensory cords and they will follow a swinging arc and bounce against his cheeks.

You will have to forgive him because he will be terribly disoriented, realizing that he should be looking ahead, but he is looking at his feet. Take him out of that dilemma by crushing his eyes against his cheeks. He will die of the shock more than likely. You will have full legal and moral rights to perform this act. It will not take any more energy expenditure than walking over and cutting off a light switch.

Have you ever heard of anything more gross or callous than this? Well, for years we gave those instructions in our demonstration and we remained uncontested. Until one afternoon at a Lions Club convention a woman sprang up in the audience and exclaimed, "And take those eyes to the eye bank!" She was a dedicated organ recruiter for the Lions Club. My whole left side went dead. The woman recruited eyes and kidneys all over her state. She would not let anyone leave the auditorium until each one of us signed away your eyes and kidneys on the back of our driver's license.

Sure it is hard and it is harsh. It borders on the macabre. However, it also represents a barrier so formidable that just on this attitude alone we will eliminate 98 percent of the problem. Imagine what courage it would take for a prowler to roam your neighborhood when he knows that this type of attitude awaits his entrance into a dwelling. There would be very few people brave (or stupid) enough to stand against this resistance.

CHAPTER NINE

Exhibitionists Could Be Nice If They Were Not So Bashful!

The national pastime of streaking has made exhibitionism almost a thing of the past. Unfortunately, there are still those terribly traumatized by their first encounter with the exhibitionist.

Exhibitionism is almost entirely an avocation of male adults. Male exhibitionists come from all walks of like. Recently one of our police officers was arrested or exposing himself in public.

Believe it or not, exhibitionists generally are introverted and shy. They are bashful. Don't attempt to hold the exhibitionist in custody unless you are prepared, physically, to do so. Let the exhibitionist go, but not get away.

Typical response to the exhibitionist is as follows: A woman walking down the street happens to glance at the guy seated in the car parked by the curb. One startled look and she averts her face, then dashes down the street. She rushes home to tell her roommate: "You should have seen what I saw today . . . no, no, I mean I had a horrible experience. This guy was seated in the car and I looked over and . . . well, I was a victim of an exhibitionist. You know what I'm trying to say?" Her roommate advises her to call the police. She responds,

"No, I couldn't do that. It would be too embarrassing."

Finally she concedes and calls the police: "Hello, police, I've just been the victim of an exhibitionist." The police: "Can you describe him, ma'am?" The woman: "Well, he was male, definitely male."

In essence, that is usually all the description the police get. Don't turn your head away: Look at him as you walk away down the street. Start at the top of his head and work down to his feet. Catch everything in between. Get a description that will identify him out of a crowd of a hundred men. If he is in a car, get the make, model, color, distinguishing marks, and license number and make sure you have the right state. Do all this while waking away from him.

If you are "flashed" while driving, then turn around and come back so you can get another look, so to speak. As soon as you can get a working description then go to the nearest phone and call the police. Give his location, then you stay in your location to meet the police for an on-the-spot identification. If he is in the area and has not seen you make the call, the police may be able to witness the guy's act firsthand (a very rare event).

Most women do not bother to report the exhibitionist. They just shrug him off and forget him along with the other mildly interesting events of the day. That's why there are so many exhibitionists working parking lots and playground areas. Some children are traumatized by the exhibitionist. Remember, take offense every time offended. Let's free ourselves of the exhibitionist nuisance. Get him off the streets. Get him out of his raincoat on sunny days.

"We had an exhibitionist in our neighborhood. He exposed himself to a woman in our neighborhood on Monday, and we all stayed home Tuesday." Now that is the attitude I am talking about. Actually what she meant was that they all locked themselves in their homes Tuesday, Wednesday, Thursday, and Friday. They communicated by phone until they decided life must return to normal because the children were getting hungry. The woman said, "I was in my backyard Saturday when I heard the crunching of grass. I whirled around and there he stood. He was in full exhibitionist garb. He had on a raincoat down to his ankles. As soon as we made eye to eye contact he dramatically flung open his coat to reveal that he wasn't even wearing socks with his shoes. It struck me as being so absurd and his movements so theatrical that I burst out laughing! I looked up to see his lips trembling and his eyes filling with tears. My reactions hurt his feelings so badly that he wrapped himself up and ran!"

CHAPTER TEN

Driving By Yourself Can Be Very Exciting!

For six blocks he has driven beside you. Every time you look over at him, he is smiling broadly and staring at you. You wonder how in the world he can drive without ever looking at the road.

What do you do with the guy who follows you everywhere?

Nothing. There really isn't much you can do. He hasn't violated any law. Ignore him. Drive on as if he doesn't exist.

If he becomes too unbearable, press your horn and keep it blowing for blocks. He will probably get embarrassed and turn off. If he doesn't, then eventually a police car will stop you to write a ticket for making a public disturbance. If you are stopped by the police, tell them what you are doing. They'll enjoy your strategy.

What if the situation is a little more serious? Say he has been following you, attempting to force you to the curb. Or maybe, even more dramatically, you suddenly realize there is someone hiding in your backseat. Whether he is on the outside or the inside, the following ploys will work.

Drive to the middle of a busy intersection and stop. Get out of your car but stay near it. Make a point to block the intersection completely, if possible. You and he will have more attention than he would ever want.

Another strategy would be to drive to a fire station and pull right inside if you can. You could also pull into the nearest gas station. It doesn't make any difference what brand they're selling; just wheel up to the pumps, get out of your car, go get yourself a candy bar, and let the service attendant have your car along with the guy in the backseat. Let it be his problem.

You're driving down a side street when you notice someone flagging you down. He is standing in the middle of the street. What should you do, stop or run him down? Stop, of course, and crack your window a little so you can hear what he has to say. If he wants a ride to the nearest service station, tell him you will go to the nearest one and direct them back to him. If he needs help then tell him you will go to a phone and make his call for him.

I personally hate the above advice. I would like to say give him a lift to where he needs to go and maybe some day someone will take a chance and do the same for you. Unfortunately a couple hundred "zeros" in this country have made it difficult for the majority of us to do what we would like to for our fellow beings. Nine out of ten times, the person claiming to need assistance is in honest need. Because of a few, past similar incidents ending in tragedy, the above advice stands. Show concern. Help the person in distress but don't let him in your car.

You are in the above situation but this time his intentions are suddenly clear. He is going to attempt to get into your car. Well, hallelujah! You needn't feel bad now; you've got him. You will never be in a more powerful position than you are when you are in the driver's seat. Even if he is two hundred and seventy pounds, six feet, six inches, and as ugly as a British bulldog, you've got him. If he is beside your car pulling on your door handle, leave your tire prints on the top of his platform shoes. If he is standing in front of your car brandishing a weapon, just race your engine and watch his fat body move (if you miss him don't back up).

Do not let anyone bluff you under any circumstances but especially when you are in the driver's seat. As long as three wheels are touching the ground, there is hardly any situation you can't get out of as long as your engine is running.

CHAPTER ELEVEN

Walking Streets, Parking Lots, Alleyways and Theater Aisles—Looking Forward to Being Attacked!

The police report cited in Chapter One stated that the woman knew she was being followed. It quoted her as saying she had such a strong suspicion she was being followed that she wanted to "take off running." As strong as her suspicion was, she never turned around to see if she truly was being followed. This is a key point.

Whenever you have the suspicion you are being followed, turn and face the possibility of being attacked. Look your follower straight in the eye. Hit him with that look you were born with, that look you can turn on and off at will, that special look you reserve for men and children. Hit him with that chilling look which is a combination of indignation, scorn, disappointment, and anger all rolled into one. Then couple that look with a harsh, deep-throated yell of, "What do you want?!!" Women have reported being followed, then turning and yelling, "What do you want?" with the result that the guy following them burst out crying!

Your attacker is walking an emotional tightrope. Show him a frightened countenance and he will attack you. He will attack because you have invited him to do so. Show him that you will not stand one action

the least bit out of line, and you will stop him dead in his tracks. It works like a miracle 98 percent of the time.

There is a whopping big 2 percent chance this technique might not work. You are walking along the street knowing you are being followed. You choose your moment, you put on your special look, and you turn on him and yell, "What do you want?!!" He looks you straight in the eye and with an adoring tone says, "Honey, I want you." You realize from his tone you have yourself a two percenter! You still have the right attitude . . . you say, "Well, not tonight, I have a headache."

If he comes toward you to seize you, thrust your fingers into vulnerable area number one—the trachea. Call an ambulance because he will need emergency treatment.

If you will go through life with the attitude, "No low-life character will spoil three minutes of my day," then he won't. Attackers are looking for easy prey. They are definitely not seeking those who will resist. Show no fear. Walk with an air of confidence. Look capable of taking care of yourself.

When in situations which cause you anxiety, display a little more bravado. Even if you are about to melt with inward fright, you must give the appearance that you can withstand the heat. Police have been using this bluff for years. They swagger through situations where there are unbelievable odds against them. Two will thrust out their chests and march into a crowd of fifty people to take out the troublemakers. Once secure and well out of sight they might throw up. Practice being brave and soon it will become a way of life. It's the only life worth living.

When He Snatches Your Purse

"Hey you so and so, that's my favorite purse!"

Now that you can hardly wait to get out on the streets and get attacked, let's say you are walking in the business district of your community displaying that air of confidence you have been practicing. You are clipping along in your dress wearing high heels and carrying a purse. All of a sudden this guy bumps you and starts pulling on your purse. You have the right attitude, "No low-life character is spoiling three minutes of my day." Heaven help the poor guy who tries anything with you! So naturally, you snatch back on the purse and wrestle him for control. Right? Wrong! Let the purse go. Separate yourself from the attacker. You have the right attitude, but holding on to the purse is the wrong strategy. Hold the purse and you will go on a one-way trip which will carry you over curbs and through flower beds, ending with you "upside a tree." Hold the purse and you may not be

lucky enough to be included in the trip. He may spin around as soon as he feels the slightest resistance and smash you in the face with his free hand. Similar scenes take place throughout this country daily.

I am not reversing my philosophy. Separate yourself from your attacker. In this situation, escape him. If you hold on to the purse, you are holding him close to you. Let him have the purse; throw it at him if you can. Notice who is doing the running this time. He is doing the footwork of your defense for you. Scream in comfort this time. Get his description!

Let the purse go but don't let him get away. Don't run after him—if you catch him, what are you going to do with him? Look well at him. Note everything, mainly those things he can't change. Do it fast because purse snatchers move like the wind. Once you have it all wrapped up in your mind, run to the phone and call the police. Borrow a coin if he has gotten away with everything you have.

Tell the police operator, "I have the description of the man who just snatched my purse." Give him a chance to react because they are certainly not used to such efficiency. The operator may finally say, "Describe him please." Your description could go something like this: "He was five feet, three inches tall and weighed 297½ pounds. He was wearing a chartreuse shirt, white pants, and orange suspenders. Those pink ballerina slippers made him have a funny little run. He had a bald spot on the back of his head with a peace sign painted in it. There was a mole under his right ear and part of the little finger on his left hand was missing." The police are quick . . . "Did you notice anything unusual about him, ma'am?" You can return, "I certainly did. He was thirty-two years old, and obviously Lithuanian. He was wearing a Mood Ring and it was green. He was carrying a darling purse."

If you called in a good description, the police really would hesitate with shock. Typically, the woman who has had her purse snatched goes home in a state of shock and confusion. She reports the offense to her family, who invite the neighbors in to commiserate. After two hours of wailing and sharing descriptions someone asks, "What did the police say?" Dawn! "I forgot to call the police!"

The police arrive two and a half hours after the purse was snatched. They take a report with a description which could fit any human being on earth and drive away in total defeat. The people in the neighborhood look after the police and say, "Why don't the police in this town ever do anything?"

Well, we are losing the battle. I don't mean we police, I mean we collectively are losing the battle. We are playing the attacker's game just the way he expects. We couldn't be doing any better for him if we all had a set of written instructions and followed them to the very letter.

Our Dwindling Freedoms

How many times have you heard the essence of the following statements?

"You don't mean you drove in that part of the city! Hasn't anyone told you that you could get killed in that section?"

"I wanted to buy a CB radio but so many have been stolen in the past few months, I said what the heck, I'm not buying some thief a radio!"

"My neighbors watch our house when we're on vacation, and we watch theirs. Only problem is, someone stole their lawn furniture one Sunday morning while we were at church. I guess you can't watch the property all the time."

"I would not dream of letting my children go to the movies by themselves."

"We bought a membership at the YMCA so we could walk around the track. We are afraid to walk in our neighborhood at night."

"Mildred, honey, could you drive to the store with me? I need some groceries and I've begun to hate driving by myself, people have gotten so bad."

"He walked up to me and said, 'Lady, give me your purse.' He had such a mean look in his eye I couldn't help but give him my purse. No, I was so frightened I didn't get a good look at him."

"He was sitting in his car and I looked down. Well, he was fully exposed."

"They drove the truck up the driveway in the middle of the day, popped the lock on the front door, loaded up the truck with every valuable in the house, and drove away."

"The man who did such a thing to a sweet old lady like her should be put under the jail."

"He said he was a doctor. He talked for fifteen minutes before I realized he was talking pure filth."

"He had a smile on his face when he walked up to me and put his hands squarely on my breast. I thought I was going to faint. He said, 'Thank you, I needed that,' and just walked away."

"I couldn't believe my eyes; She was taking a coat off the rack and stuffing it into a bag. I watched her walk to a counter, pick up a scarf, take it to the checkout register, pay only for the scarf and walk out. I would never have such nerve. Report it? Are you kidding? That woman would find out who I am and come into my house and kill me! Whew!! Report it? You must be crazy."

"Now that we have moved to Camelot Village, I feel much safer. There is a guard at our gate who makes us show him our ID cards every time we enter. Sure it takes a little time, but it is worth it."

"I don't mind being frisked like this before boarding the plane; knowing everyone has been frisked makes me feel like I might get to my destination."

"It was so sad seeing that young family stranded on the road way out nowhere. But you know how many people have been robbed when they stopped to assist people on the road."

"Olive, if you don't stop speaking to strangers as you do, I will have to stop going to town with you. You know how many perverts there are in this town. You are inviting trouble every time you smile at a stranger."

"Sensitive, that's not the word for it. This alarm system goes off every time the wind blows. The police? No, they don't seem to mind, but it does seem like it is taking them longer to get here each time the alarm goes off. It only cost $1,500. For our peace of mind it would have been cheap at twice the price."

Sound familiar?

These statements are the expression of the national attitude. With this attitude, it is no wonder there is such a crime problem in this country. We are inviting aggression every day of our lives. The monumental loss of freedom implied by these statements is staggering. Think about it! Walking in your neighborhood at day's end, children going to the neighborhood movie house unaccompanied, driving to a shopping center by yourself, sitting in the park reading a book, answering the phone without the feeling of dread, leaving your front door unlocked while visiting a neighbor, being able to smile at a stranger on the street and even chance wishing him a good day, sleeping with your windows open at night. All are freedoms that have been lost already by millions of people because of their all-encompassing fear. The above list is merely representative of lost freedoms. The list could go on for another three pages. Make your own list, but let me warn you; it will make you sick.

Encourage your friends and associates to make a list of freedoms lost through fear and apprehension. Recently, I read a book on self-protection which listed so many "do nots" that the only alternative was to lock yourself in a barricaded house and raise your own food. One of the tips on protection went so far as to advise, "While working in the front yard make sure the back door is locked." If the situation has degenerated to a point where the back door must be locked while we are in the front of our property, then things have gone far enough. How much further can we be pushed? Not much further because we are near the end of the road.

Weakness invites exploitation. Fear works like a self-fulfilling prophecy where all things feared will eventuate. We have to look forward to being attacked. We all must take offense every time offended. When any one of us in this country is offended, we are all offended. When one person is attacked, we are all being attacked. We frightened law-abiding citizens have given the law violator enormous control over our lives. We must reverse this control, which is entirely self-induced.

Happily, in the last year I have noticed a change in attitude evidenced by the women who attend my self-defense demonstrations. Some are finally expressing outrage over the state of crime in the community. They feel something has to be done and are now willing to be part of reversing the trend. There is no alternative. If we continue to withdraw, they will get stronger. There is no isolating ourselves from the problem; it has been allowed to go too far. We have "pulled the blanket over our heads" but it did not go away.

Can there ever be a place in this country where we can accept the idea we cannot travel in safety? Never! When we hear of such a place we must all go there and defy whoever is causing the fear to spoil three minutes of our day.

The laws do not restrict our freedom, they insure our freedom. It is the lack of law enforcement that is causing 98 percent of the people of this country to lose their freedom. An unorganized, motley crew of isolated individuals is accomplishing what no nation on earth could ever hope to achieve; they are making us submit.

Demand your rights to travel free of fear. Take offense every time offended. Insist that the laws be enforced. Don't go down without fighting—you'll hate yourself if you do.

But What If He Has a Weapon?

The gun in his hand is the size of a cannon. He says, "Give me that purse." Toss the purse to him. Say, "I have thirty-seven cents in that purse but if you will take a minute I will be happy to write you a check."

A lot of people have successfully defended property. They have sent robbers running down the street. A woman in her mid-sixties parked her car in one of those downtown parking lots where they trust you to put the money in the meter. There was no attendant. Before she could get out of her car a man opened the door and pointed a gun at her chest. He angled his body so only she could see the gun. He said, "Give me that purse!" She said, "I will not! I work hard for my money. Why don't you get out and get a job like everyone else?" He looked down at his gun to make sure it was still there. He just couldn't believe what he was hearing. He repeated, "Lady, give me that purse!" This time she really started berating him. He backed off, covered his gun, and said, "Lady, will you let me apologize?" She said, "I will not!" He took off running and she started chasing him. He rounded the corner of a building to pass out of her sight. She stopped and thought to herself, "What am I going to do with him when I catch him?"

This resistance might work more times than you could ever imagine but the gamble is too great. You would be gambling with your person against the value of the property you are defending. There is no property equal to the value of your person. Let the property go but do not let him get away. Get a description that will tag him perfectly. "Male with a gun" is not too complete a description. The gun will be in his pocket as soon as he leaves you and you will have described 455,000 suspects in your community.

The gun in his hand is the size of a cannon but this time he says, "Honey, I love the way you look tonight. Get in this car. If you say one word I will blow your face off!"

"Blow your face off?" What a horrible expression. And you noticed that when he said it, he did not have the slightest quiver in his voice. His hand did not tremble and his tone was terribly dictatorial. He means "get in the car."

Now it is a matter of person, not property. Turn your back on his weapon and walk away. Look over your shoulder and say, "Drop dead." Will he shoot you? He might. But if he does, you have just missed a lot of unpleasantness in between, because he was going to kill you anyway. If you go with him to the cozy cornfield that he has chosen for you and become his victim as well as his only witness, it will make more sense for him to kill you than to release you. Since that is universally the case, make your attacker kill you on the street corner or in the parking lot. Wherever his approach has a public aspect to it, you can turn your back on your attacker and walk away scot-free. Don't carry the stance to the extreme and say, "Yan, yan, a yan, yan, shoot me, shoot me, shoot me" while you are thumbing your nose at him. There are certain strange ones who will shoot you because they don't like your act.

Never try any of the above with husband or boyfriend. They will blow your head off. People are killed by loved ones, not strangers. Look up the statistics. Loved ones are emotionally involved with you. Strangers are not.

You have just stepped from your automobile. You have not even had a chance to close the door. He stands in front of you with a knife pressed toward your breast. He says, "Get back in the car, we have places to drive." You can't even back off because the door blocks you. You are blocked to your right by the car door. You sure don't want to go forward and impale yourself on his knife. He wants you back in the car so you certainly don't want to follow those instructions. So where can you go? Sit down on the pavement.

You look up into his eyes and tell him softly in volume but firmly in tone, "I don't want you to kill me. Please don't hurt me. But I am not going with you. I am not leaving this spot. Now just go away and find someone else." Will he go away? Yes. If he doesn't? If he kills you? Bad luck! Just one of those rotten days.

"Lieutenant, how about all those women we hear about who are carried from the parking lot to the cozy cornfield, criminally assaulted, and returned back to the parking lot? How about all of those women we read about who are carried across the state line, criminally assaulted, and then returned back to their home address to be let out at their driveway? The attacker drives away with a wave of thanks and appreciation. They were not killed. They were just raped! Why are you urging us to force the attacker to make a kill-or-release decision? In fact, I read that most women who were criminally assaulted were not killed. Some may have been badly beaten but they were not killed. Isn't it wiser to submit than to be killed?"

This argument, which I hear every day of my life, is meant to be an argument against what I am urging you to do but it is actually an argument for my stand. If the attacker releases his victim, he releases a witness who will shadow his freedom the rest of his life. There is no statute of limitations for rape (at this writing). The victim could spot her attacker ten years after the crime and have him arrested. He knows this. Yet he still releases his victim.

If the attacker does not kill a victim who means so much to him, will he kill the woman who turns and walks away? Will he kill the woman seated on the parking lot? This woman means nothing to him. She is the threat of a misdemeanor charge and nothing more. He knows that and he will not kill her. If he does, he was going to kill her anyway.

Make him kill you on the parking lot rather than the cornfield. It is more convenient for those who will have to find you. It will be better for your family and loved ones. They will suffer less agony if you are found immediately rather than having to wait for you to be discovered hidden beneath a pile of cornstalks. Think about it. Never go with your attacker.

Too Many of the Right People Have the Wrong Attitude

We are being preconditioned to be victims. That conditioning is taking place every day of our lives. It is coming at us from every angle. It comes at us from police departments, rape crisis people, security firms, safety councils, churches, and the worst offenders of all: loved ones. This conditioning is not taking place through some malintent or communist plot but through the most well-meaning of motivations. In some of the Memphis Police Department's crime prevention programs where crime prevention tips were being given I came close to saying things like: "Never park your car." "Do not leave your house after six P.M." "Avoid all neighborhoods populated by people." And one that actually was advised: "Travel in packs!" These well-intentioned tips were stealing the streets away from the citizen and giving them to the attackers.

In the past ten years people have been made to feel guilty for being victimized. Have you heard of charges like: "Well, lady if you locked your car door could he have stolen it that easily?" "Lady, were you dressed then as you are now? No wonder you were attacked. I feel like attacking you myself. You need to put some clothes on." "Well, you will have to admit that your teenage daughter is rather well endowed." "Nine o'clock at night in this hospital parking lot, what did you expect? Come back here next week at nine o'clock and you will be attacked again. There are just some places you will have to learn that you can't go after a certain hour." "Ma'am, would you mind walking out in your front yard for just a moment? There is something I would like to show you. Look next door. The lady's house next door was not burglarized. Why did your burglar choose your house and not hers? Could it be that tall chain-link fence out front? Maybe the big ugly dog behind that fence? Look at each one of her windows. The shades are pulled and each window has steel bars. Her front door obviously has not been opened in five years. Your house is a sieve. Burglars can flow through your house at will!" "If you had watched your child properly on that playground he would not have been molested."

Have you heard of those charges or similar ones? Of course you have. They are an everyday part of our lives. This type of thinking sanctions the crime problem. These charges are part of the national attitude which says that if you have not taken the proper precautions to protect yourself or your property, then the attacker or thief has a right to proceed with his unlawful act. This type of thinking is unreasonable, illogical, and in my opinion obscene. It makes me choke. I want to scream, Listen to what you are saying! You are saying that if you have not locked your car then the thief may (not can but *may*) steal it. If a woman wants to wear shorts then she has to face the consequences of an attacker's lust. If the child matures early toward womanhood then we have to expect her to be attacked. Stay out of this section of the city because it belongs to the attacker. Don't take the alleyway because we have officially designated this shortcut as attacker's territory. To really be safe I think you had best raise those vegetables in your bedroom. And it goes on and on and on!!!

I have had hundreds of success stories shared with me where women have foiled their attackers by just determining not to be the victim. One such story that I am very proud of illustrates two very important points. I am proud of this story because the young lady who shared it with me gave me credit for her attitude.

This young lady told me that while she was living at home with her parents she had the following experience. One evening around ten o'clock she felt the need for a before-bedtime snack. She wanted some milk and cookies. She found that there was no milk for that evening or for the morning. She decided that she would surprise her parents and voluntarily go to the nearest store to buy the milk on her own. It was a lovely night so she walked the two blocks to the convenience store. She was halfway back to her house when a carload of six young men pulled to the curb beside her. The fellow on the passenger side opened his door, put one foot out of the car, and said, "Honey, you are going to give the six of us a good time tonight." Before he could even get out of the car she rushed toward him with the milk bottle raised above her head yelling, "You had just better try something like that with me!" She said the driver of the car accelerated away so fast that it left the fellow who had made the approach to her hanging half in and half out of the car. She said she watched him seesaw up and down for two blocks trying to get back in the car.

Point number one is that her determination not to be a victim worked like a miracle. It was easy. She was thrilled with the success of her defiance and rushed home to share the thrill with her parents. Point number two is that the parents were not equally thrilled. They were appalled that she had the "stupidity" to go out on the streets at ten o'clock at night. They warned her never to do that again because she would always be attacked at that time of night in her neighborhood.

Don't let anyone talk you into giving your streets to the attacker. That young lady probably could take that same walk every night for the next twenty years and not be approached or bothered. The neighborhood in which her incident occurred is one of the safest in her city. With her attitude it will always be a safe neighborhood. With her parents' attitude it will soon become too dangerous to walk through in the daytime.

It Truly Is Just a Matter of Attitude

No one has a right to steal your car, to break into your house, to whisper obscenities in your ear on the phone, or to shout them at you as you cross the street. No one has a right to offend you in any way. Take offense every time offended.

This attitude transcends human experience and extends into the realm of all living creatures. Have you ever seen a kitten chase a dog? I have. One afternoon I saw a bull terrier run across a yard to chew up a little kitten. The kitten saw that there was no possible escape from the dog. The kitten bristled its back and hissed through clenched teeth. It was like the cartoons. The dog went into the skids and turned around to yelp away. The little kitten was so proud of herself she just pranced all over the yard the rest of the day.

Have you ever seen a mouse chase a human being? I am not talking about a rat—but a tiny little mouse. A little mouse with no avenue of escape will rear up on its little haunches and expose its tiny little claws to strike at the oncoming danger. People will run out of the house! All you have to do is walk over to the little mouse and step on it. It will be gone. But no one does that. When the mouse takes that stand of resistance people will run from it. If that attitudinal stand will work for a tiny little mouse, will it not work for a nation?!